CONQUERING FEAR

© 2022 Christ for all Nations
Printed in the UK
Edition 1, Printing 1

G000231660

Scripture quotations are taken from:

New King James Version of the Bible, copyright © 1979, 1980, 1982, Thomas Nelson, Inc., Publishers. Used with permission, all rights reserved worldwide.

The Amplified Bible ®, NASB ® New Testament, copyright © 1958, 1987, by The Lockman Foundation, La Habra, California. Used by permission www.Lockman.org

The Amplified Bible, Old Testament, copyright © 1964, 1987 by Zondervan Publishing House, Grand Rapids, Michigan. Used by permission www.Lockman.org

The Holy Bible, New International Version® NIV®, copyright © 1973 1978 1984 2011 by Biblica, Inc. TM Used with permission, all rights reserved worldwide.

Slaying Dragons by Daniel Kolenda, (Lake Mary, Florida, copyright © Charisma Media/Charisma House Book Group 2019) Used by permission.

Evangelism by Fire by Reinhard Bonnke, (Lake Mary, Florida, copyright © Charisma Media/Charisma House Book Group 2011) Used by permission.

Live Before you die by Daniel Kolenda, (Lake Mary, Florida, copyright © Charisma Media/Charisma House Book Group 2013) Used by permission.

Excerpted from Daily Fire Devotional:365 Days in Gods Word by Reinhard Bonnke, © 2015 by Reinhard Bonnke. Published by Whitaker House, New Kensington, PA. Used with permission. All rights reserved. www.whitakerhouse.com

Faith: The link with God's power by Reinhard Bonnke (Harvester Services 2013) Used with permission.

Unlocking the Miraculous by Daniel Kolenda (Orlando, Florida, copyright © Christ for all Nations 2016)

Surviving your Wilderness by Daniel Kolenda (Orlando, Florida, copyright © Christ for all Nations 2016)

Taking Action by Reinhard Bonnke (Lake Mary, Florida, copyright © Charisma Media/Charisma House Book Group 2012)

Visit the www.cfan.org.uk

ISBN: 978-3-96431-026-2

INTRODUCTION

This book came about as a response to the wave of fear and uncertainty that swept over the world in 2020, as we all came to grips with a pandemic. Christians all over the globe were faced with the same questions and challenges. Why is this happening? How will my family and I come through this? Does God have a plan in this time? What can I do about this fear that I'm feeling?

There are answers for these questions! There's a path for every single Christian that leads out of the valley, out of fear, and into victory and faith. In your hands is a fear-busting, faith-building, Holy-Spirit-equipping 60-day Bible study, with excerpts from bestselling books by Evangelist Reinhard Bonnke and me.

Take these messages, put them into action, and let God make you CONQUER FEAR!

Evangelist Daniel Kolenda
President – Christ for all Nations

GETTING STRONGER!

We are living in remarkable times. The entire world is gripped by fear and uncertainty. I don't know all the answers, but there are some things we can know for sure. As children of God we have access to a peace that passes understanding – that is, it is not natural or carnal. It is supernatural, surpassing what the mind and intellect can comprehend. That is important because what we need right now is not more information – we are always being bombarded with news. What we need is something that goes straight into the core of our being and fortifies us from within. That is what the Word of God does. In this book, over the next 60 days, I am going to bombard your heart and mind with timeless, unchangeable truth from God's Word that will act like a heavenly vaccine, inoculating you against fear, anxiety and worry.

Some people begin to waver in times like these. Some question God, His Word, His love and His faithfulness. But this is the time we need to cling to Him as never before. I remember an exchange Reinhard Bonnke once had with a man who was sick and suffering. The man said he was having "a crisis of faith." Reinhard said, "My brother, when you are drowning, that is the worst time to let go of the lifeline." If you are struggling, grab a hold of God's Word and His truth with all your might – it is your lifeline!

Jesus says in John 10:10, *"The thief comes only to steal and kill and destroy. I came that they may have life and have it abundantly."*

The Lord made a clear contrast between His mission and the devil's mission. Satan's plans for us are in complete opposition to God's plans for us! It is paramount we believe this foundational truth: Jesus came that we may have life and have it abundantly!

We see the declarations of His love for mankind all over the Scriptures, both in His words and in His actions – and most profoundly, when He laid down His life for us on the cross. Jesus loves us! He is for us! He gave us His word as our solid rock to stand on, so that when the thief comes to attack, we can stand in unwavering trust on God's faithful promises. Often, what makes people susceptible to an attack of the enemy, is the onset of doubt and unbelief in the goodness of God and the truth of His word. Immunity, on the other hand, is the lack of susceptibility, especially to something unwelcome or harmful. Satan knows He has no legal right to steal, kill, and destroy you, unless he can persuade you to hand over to him your God-given power and authority as sons and daughters of God. The devil plots and schemes to deceive the masses by planting false accusations, twisting the truth, and most often, by employing fear tactics. He uses fear because it tends to work so well on the wavering. Ultimately, those who succumb to unbelief help him accomplish his mission. Once Satan has convinced a person to misplace their trust in the Lord, then they become susceptible to the contagions of fear, doubt, and unbelief. The way to become immune to these attacks from the enemy, is to hold fast in unwavering faith in Jesus and his word. In the days ahead, we are going to press into the truth, so that we can stand firm against all attacks, securely fortified in the victory we have in Jesus!

When a person is exposed to a pathogen and they survive, their bodies learn how to fight that contagion and they become immune to it from then on. This is where we get the old cliché, "what doesn't kill you makes you stronger." I believe it is very similar with our spirits. As we go through life, overcoming trials and difficulties, emerging victorious, walking hand-in-hand with Jesus, we become stronger, spiritually tougher and more resilient in faith. That is why a difficult, challenging season is so important. It can be a training ground for the more significant battles to come in the future. Jeremiah asked, *"If you have raced with men on foot and they have worn you out, how can you compete with horses? If you stumble in safe country, how will you manage in the thickets by the Jordan?"* (Jer. 12:5)

Join me for the next 60-days as we confront the pathogen of fear head on and eradicate it with the antidote of God's Word. May God use this season in all of our lives to build unwavering trust in our hearts for Him as never before.

written it is written it is written it is written it is writ
written it is written it is written it is written it is writ
written it is written it is written it is written it is writ
written it is written it is written it is written it is writ
written it is written it is written it is written it is writ
written it is

"IT IS WRITTEN!"

Do you ever notice that sometimes it seems as if you're on a spiritual high? You're tangibly feeling the presence of God, receiving fresh revelation, the anointing is flowing like oil, and you're clearly hearing the Lord speaking to your spirit. Then other times, it seems as though the heavens are brass, the oil has run dry, and if the anointing is there – *you* certainly can't tell! You didn't get a single goose bump during praise and worship. Not one tear dropped, not one hair raised.

During those moments when the thrills of His glory have lifted, and you find yourself in a spiritual valley, you may be tempted to question what you encountered when you were on the mountaintop. You may be tempted by the devil to fear that what you experienced previously wasn't real. You see, if we base our faith in our feelings, then our faith will fluctuate whenever they do.

When Satan came to tempt Jesus in the desert (Matthew 4:1-11) he said, *"If you are the Son of God, command these stones to become loaves of bread."* The word, "if" is so subtle and so small, yet such a huge stumbling block to many, because in that one little word, one's entire belief system can be shaken. This is why we must follow the Lord's example and refuse to rely on our feelings or current experiences, especially when facing the temptation of doubt.

Jesus responded, *"It is written, 'Man shall not live by bread alone, but by every word that comes from the mouth of God.'"* (Matthew 4:4) Every time Jesus responded to the devil, He said, *"It is written..."* Jesus stood on the word of God, and we must do the same. It's our sure foundation! It doesn't matter what the circumstances are, or what the 'ifs' are, or how we are feeling in any given moment – the word of God must have the final say in every season of our lives.

The following is a list of scriptures that I would encourage you to read aloud and to confess over yourself and your family. Read them again and again until you sense faith and courage arising in your heart. This was the ammunition Jesus used against Satan in the wilderness ("it is written") and it will be your strength as well:

IT IS WRITTEN:
"And my God will meet all your needs according to the riches of his glory in Christ Jesus" (Phil. 4:19).

IT IS WRITTEN:
"He will call on me, and I will answer him" (Ps. 91:15).

IT IS WRITTEN:
"The one who sows righteousness reaps a sure reward" (Prov. 11:18).

IT IS WRITTEN:
"If that is how God clothes the grass of the field, which is here today and tomorrow is thrown into the fire, will he not much more clothe you—you of little faith?" (Matt. 6:30).

IT IS WRITTEN:
"I have given you authority to trample on snakes and scorpions and to overcome all the power of the enemy; nothing will harm you" (Luke 10:19).

IT IS WRITTEN:
"No harm will overtake you, no disaster will come near your tent" (Ps. 91:10).

IT IS WRITTEN:
"The righteous person may have many troubles, but the Lord delivers him from them all" (Ps. 34:19).

IT IS WRITTEN:
"And the prayer offered in faith will make the sick person well; the Lord will raise them up" (Jas. 5:15).

IT IS WRITTEN:
"Cast your cares on the Lord, and he will sustain you; he will never let the righteous be shaken" (Ps. 55:22).

IT IS WRITTEN:
"The angel of the Lord encamps around those who fear him, and he delivers them" (Ps. 34:7).

IT IS WRITTEN:
"Commit your way to the Lord; trust in him and he will do this" (Ps. 37:5).

IT IS WRITTEN:
"He settles the childless woman in her home as a happy mother of children" (Ps. 113:9).

IT IS WRITTEN:
"His mercy endures forever" (Ps. 136:1).

IT IS WRITTEN:
"We are hard pressed on every side, but not crushed; perplexed, but not in despair; persecuted, but not abandoned; struck down, but not destroyed" (2 Cor. 4:8–9).

THE VICTORY THAT HAS OVERCOME THE WORLD!

The Bible says, *"For God has not given us a spirit of fear, but of power, and of love and of a sound mind."* (2 Timothy 1:7)

This scripture makes it clear that the spirit of fear is not from God. When danger threatens us, fear tries to latch onto us. Even our body chemistry changes when we sense impending disaster, when our circumstances are doom and gloom, or when pain becomes overwhelming, and our natural response is to be alarmed and fearful.

So, what does a spirit of power, love, and a sound mind do in the face of fear? It removes fear's death grip that tries to paralyze us. Fear can come, but it cannot bind those who belong to the Lord because we are overcomers!

"For everyone who has been born of God overcomes the world. And this is the victory that has overcome the world – our faith." (1 John 5:4)

"Fear not, for I am with you; be not dismayed, for I am your God; I will strengthen you, I will help you, I will uphold you with my righteous right hand." (Isaiah 40:10)

Jesus said, *"Do not be afraid; only believe"* (Luke 8:50).

The Bible's greatest illustration of fear and unbelief lasted forty years with the tribes of Israel in the wilderness. Even though their wanderings took them close to the border of the Promised Land, they did not actually believe they could cross over because they had already succumbed to fear. The disease of fear had enveloped what little faith was in their hearts. Their faith was useless for as long as they feared, which is why most of them never reached the Promised Land. They complained about their situation but did not have enough faith to change it.

Moses sent twelve spies from each head of the tribes of Israel to spy out the land of Canaan as the Lord had commanded (Numbers 13). There were two very different reports when they returned. This resulted in ten of them falling prey to unbelief and discouragement, and two full of faith with courage to move forward and possess the land. This is probably a normal average – two out of twelve believe and get what God has for them. The rest only wish for it and die, never taking hold of it. There will always be more of those who are full of fear than those who are full of faith. Which will you choose to be?

THE WORD IS OUR
SOURCE OF FAITH!

Jesus specializes in troubleshooting every type of problem known to mankind! He is our Lord and Savior, our provider, our healer, our shepherd, our advocate, and our great defender... I could go on and on! There is no problem too big for Him to solve! You're never going to come to Him with an urgent prayer request and hear Him reply, "Oh no! That's terrible news! What ever shall I do?" There is literally no issue He cannot solve!

Oftentimes, if we are allowing fear to creep into our thought life, it's because we have not been meditating on the Word of God. Jesus can do anything! *"For nothing will be impossible with God."* (Luke 1:37)

I cannot emphasize this enough – the word of God is the most valuable tool we have. The only answer for the whole world is found in the Bible. Many people remain in a continual state of fear. For some it would seem that irrevocable disaster and destruction are lurking around every corner, and yet the entire Bible is all about God's plan of mercy, redemption, and restoration for mankind.

For those who belong to Christ, there is nothing to fear – there is only good news!

The antidote to fear is faith. You know, the Bible was written for people with no actual faith. Meaning, we all begin with a minus, in terms of faith. If we have no faith, reading the Bible will produce it; if we have some faith, reading the Bible will produce more! We do not first acquire the faith that we bring to Scripture. Scripture produces, encourages, and grows our faith!

Romans 10:17 says, *"So then, faith comes by hearing, and hearing by the word of God."* I encourage you to ask the Holy Spirit to guide you in God's Word and reveal the truth to you as you read through your Bible. Then hone in on the verses that catch your attention. Many times, the Scriptures that seem to "pop out" to us are the ones He wants us to meditate on.

And as we meditate on His word, faith begins to arise in our hearts!

FAITH WITHOUT QUESTIONS OR QUALIFIERS!

Fear and unbelief are not intellectual responses, but emotional responses of the heart from a lack of faith in God. Meaning the root of unbelief isn't in the mind, but in the heart.

Unfortunately, "faith" has become a religious generalization. Authentic faith is accepting the credibility of God – *"He who promised is faithful"* (Heb. 10:23). Faith means we leave things up to Jesus, step out in trust, and obey Him at His word. "Trust in the Lord," is a foundational biblical principle, and that should be followed by the attitude, *"Though He slay me, yet will I trust Him"* (Job 13:15).

Jesus expects us to trust Him with this kind of attitude and response. How do we know this?

Well, He made the most striking statement in the book of Luke: *"They will put some of you to death. And you will be hated by all for my name's sake. But not a hair of your head shall be lost"* (Luke 21:16-18).

He expects our trust no matter what the outcome. Faith is not merely showing approval for Scripture or being an expert on doctrine. We can be biblically correct, but void of any real trust in God. Faith is childlike trust in Jesus and full surrender of our lives to Him. For example, putting qualifiers on prayers like, "I'll believe in You, God, if You answer this prayer," shows a gross ignorance of the whole understanding of what faith is.

You see, God does not always do what we think He should do. In fact, that is why we have to trust Him! If He always answered every prayer in the way and timing we wanted, faith would not be necessary. Also, we must remember that God is God, and we are not. If we demand to know why God does or does not do something as a condition for our trust, then we do not have true faith. God accepts no terms for our trust in Him. He is the creator of the Universe! He does not conform to the pattern of our small thinking in order to convince us to believe. If we do not believe, it is always our loss, not His. May we never doubt in God or in His goodness towards us.

Hebrews 11:6 says, *"And without faith it is impossible to please Him, for whoever would draw near to God must believe that He exists and that He rewards those who diligently seek Him."* Also, Psalms 34:8 says, "Oh, taste and see that the Lord is good; blessed is the man who trusts in Him!" When we fully believe that He exists, He is good, and He loves us, all the qualifiers and questions fall away.

Like a child in the arms of his father, we are able to find rest for our souls. *"He who dwells in the shelter of the Most High will abide in the shadow of the Almighty. I will say to the Lord, 'My refuge and my fortress, my God, in whom I trust.'"* (Psalm 91:1-2)

THE FEAR OF THE LORD

In the Bible we learn some fear is good and some is bad. The books of Psalms and Proverbs speak of "the fear of the Lord" as a virtue fourteen times! *"The fear of the Lord is the beginning of wisdom"* (Psalm 111:10), *"a fountain of life"* (Proverbs 14:27), and *"riches and honor and life"* (Proverbs 22:4). Yet 1 John 4:18 says, *"Fear involves torment. But he who fears has not been made perfect in love."* In Exodus 20:20, we find both aspects: *"Do not fear; for God has come to test you, and that His fear may be before you, so that you may not sin."*

How can fear be both good and bad? The answer depends on what or whom we fear. To fear God is a wholesome attitude! When we fear the devil, it is a sign we do not fear God, which means we have no faith in God. In fact, to fear Satan is to have faith in Satan! However, when we fear the Lord, we are essentially saying, "Ultimately Lord, You are in control. Therefore, my life is in Your capable hands, and I submit to You!"

On the other hand, to fear Satan, is to believe he's in control, your life is in his hands and you submit to him... May it never be so! Having the fear of the Lord keeps unhealthy worries from growing into monstrous trepidations, because it reveals to us Jesus' supreme position as King of Kings and Lord of Lords. The fear of the Lord keeps us in alignment with the truth! Satan would delight in nothing more, than for your perspective of divine supremacy to get twisted. He wants your focus to get off of the Lord, and onto Him.

The devil would love for you to believe that he calls all the shots and your life is susceptible to his plans for your destruction. But Jesus defeated him once and for all on the cross! Hallelujah! The finished work of the cross is not only a sign of the Lord's victory over Satan – but your victory over him as well! Be encouraged! Proverbs 19:23 says,

"The fear of the Lord leads to life, so that one may sleep satisfied, untouched by evil."

Those who have the good fear – the fear of the Lord, are untouchable!

THE NAME ABOVE ALL NAMES!

We believe and proclaim that Jesus is the name above all other names. Therefore, it is important for us to know what is in His name. We begin to find out by looking at the great name of God, the Lord (Yahweh). Israel held that name as sacred and awesome. At the beginning, it was only a title, like a sealed book. They did not know what was in it. It held the mystery of God's very being, a holy secret. Even Moses had to ask what it was, and God's answer was simply, *"I am who I am"* (Exodus 3:14). Who He was, had not yet been revealed. However, *"He made known His ways to Moses, His acts to the children of Israel"* (Psalm 103:7).

Then, *"precept upon precept, line upon line"* (Isaiah 28:10), the Lord opened His glory to Israel. Name was added to name, but His greatest name was not yet known. It would not be a mere title or a mystery but a great explanation. It would not be known until it was understood in all its wonder, height, and depth. It is the mighty name of Jesus! *"Therefore God also has highly exalted Him and given Him the name which is above every name, that at the name of Jesus every knee should bow, of those in heaven, and of those on earth, and of those under the earth, and that every tongue should confess that Jesus Christ is Lord, to the glory of God the Father"* (Philippians 2:9 – 11).

I declare over you today that the name of Jesus is above fear.

The name of Jesus is above lack.

The name of Jesus is above disease.

The name of Jesus is above loneliness.

The name of Jesus is above depression.

The name of Jesus is above loss.

The name of Jesus is above uncertainty.

The name of Jesus is above death.

The name of Jesus is above _____.
(you fill in the blank – what is weighing on your heart and mind).

Declare it today in faith!
The name of Jesus is the name above
all names!

A WEAPON AGAINST FEAR

Purpose is a powerful weapon against fear. What gave thousands of young men the courage to storm the beaches of Normandy on June 6, 1944, also known as D-Day? They were fortified by purpose – to confront and conquer a great evil. In our lives we will find the same truth. When we are living with great purpose, we are filled with courage. If we can remember that time is short and, as Christians, we have been entrusted with a heavenly assignment – to storm the gates of Hell, to win the lost and to set the captives free – this purpose will fill us with courage.

"Little children, it is the last hour" (1 John 2:18). I know it seems that this hour has lasted for a very long time. John

wrote those words over nineteen centuries ago. Do not let that observation confuse you. We can be certain of one thing—if it was the last hour then, it most certainly is now! If John were writing today, he probably would write,

"Little children, it is the last second of the last minute of the last hour."

Most people live as if this life were a permanent arrangement. Often, it is only in the face of a crisis or a calamity that they are awakened to the fact that their days are numbered. *"A person's days are determined; you have decreed the number of his months and have set limits he cannot exceed"* (Job 14:5).

Our days are numbered. There is actually only time for the important things. I am thinking about the church of Jesus Christ in particular. People often point out that life consists of a thousand details, but the minor must not outweigh the major. The church is to concern itself with one aim - to live on fire for Jesus and campaign for souls. When Scripture proclaims, "It is the last hour," it truly is. For the message of the Gospel, it is always the last hour. This unique, special doctrine of Scripture is called "imminence."

Many sit back and relax, thinking that there are still four months to the harvest (John 4:35). If you want to know how a single individual like Paul did so much, read his open letter to the Corinthians. He lived as if the end of all things was at hand, as if the final curtain was always imminent. *"But this I say, brethren, the time is short, so that from now on even those who have wives should be as though they had none, those who weep, as though they did not weep, those who rejoice as though they did not rejoice, those who buy as though they did not possess, and those who use this world, as*

not misusing it. For the form of this world is passing away"
(1 Corinthians 7:29-31).

The Gospel is eternal, but we do not have eternity to preach it. It seems as though we have that long when we view the leisurely operations of the church on the Gospel front. We have only as long as we live to reach those who live as long as we live. Today, nearly eight billion souls are alive on this planet. They are not in a future age that will need to be evangelized, but present and living now on earth. It is the last hour.

Luke 21:11 says, *"There will be great earthquakes, and in various places famines and pestilences. And there will be terrors and great signs from heaven."* So, what then will we do as the clock races towards the end and chaos, terror, famines and plagues increase in the earth? We can busy ourselves with the fear that the media sells us, focusing inward on frantically preserving our lives and our interests, OR we can busy ourselves with the great commission, focusing outward, forsaking our lives and our interests for the sake of the Gospel being preached throughout the earth! We can choose to be paralyzed in fear, or be about the Father's business, faithfully advancing His kingdom in whichever ways we are able.

Right now, you may not see yourself in a position to do much for the Lord. But that is exactly what the enemy of your soul wants you to believe! Satan would love for the church to believe that the proclamation of the Gospel and the ministry of Jesus Christ is on. But that couldn't be further from the truth! Jesus is always two steps ahead of Satan and three on Sunday. In fact, the advancement of the kingdom of God is only picking up the pace!

We have so much more connection right now to our families and loved ones through the modern technologies we have today. The field is ripe for harvest! I encourage you to ask the Lord how you can be on active duty in the Gospel brigade today. There may be someone sitting under your own roof that needs to know the love of Jesus. There may be a friend or a relative that you haven't had time to catch up with lately – now is the time for that phone call! Today is the day of salvation!

When you give, you reap the same reward as the sower because you enable the seed to be spread, and spread much further than it could ever go without your support. And finally, but most certainly not the least important, you can pray! You can pray for the harvest... *"Therefore pray earnestly to the Lord of the harvest to send out laborers into his harvest"* (Matthew 9:38). I'm encouraged by the Holy Spirit of this fact:

Nothing of importance to heaven has ever been put on the back burner. May we be found faithful, not fearful, and may the lamb receive the reward for His suffering.

THE REMEDY!

Evangelist Reinhard Bonnke once shared a story about a man who told him that he also was a "spiritual counselor." However, the man did not believe that Jesus Christ is the Son of God, nor that the Bible is the Word of God. Reinhard wondered how this "counselor" counseled anybody, so he asked, "Do they come to you, and then go away with broken hearts?" "Oh no," the man assured him, "I just calm them down." Reinhard looked him in the eye and said, "Mister, a man on a sinking ship needs more than a tranquilizer. Don't calm him down. He is going down already! When Jesus comes to a man in a shipwreck, He doesn't throw him a Valium pill and say, 'Perish in peace.' He reaches down His nail-scarred hand, grips him, lifts him, and says to him, *'Because I live, you will live also!'"* (John 14:19). This is the Gospel of Jesus Christ that must be preached! Jesus is the Savior of our world. He alone is the calm to all fears! His message is life, peace, hope, and health for the spirit, soul, and body! The Gospel is the remedy!

The book of Luke, chapter 4 describes the day that Jesus stood up in a synagogue full of people, to read from the book of Isaiah. He said, *"The Spirit of the Lord is upon Me, because He anointed Me to preach the gospel to the poor. He has sent Me to proclaim release to the captives, and recovery of sight to the blind, to set free those who are oppressed, to proclaim the favorable year of the Lord"* (Luke 4:16-19). This is "the favorable year of the Lord."

In every nation, the enslaved abound – slaves to every contemptible habit, slaves to fear, slaves to doubt, slaves to depression. The devil never lets anyone out on parole. Everywhere people are failure-prone, sin-prone, morally defective, and spiritually bound. But the jubilee trumpet has already sounded! The price of their freedom has been paid. This is what we must preach, because people have forgotten it. They have forgotten that Christ has come, and what that actually means for us.

This is not the pre-Christian era. We are not waiting for Christ to come and conquer. The war is already over! Freedom is ours! Jesus opened the kingdom of liberty and blew the trumpet of emancipation when He cried on the cross, *"It is finished!"* People who should know better are calling this the "post-Christian" era. As if the work of Christ was only for a past age! That certainly is not true. Christ opened prison doors forever, not just for a certain period in the past. The work of Jesus cannot be exhausted or undone. It is the greatest redemptive force at work on the earth today. Never again can prison doors be bolted on human beings. When Jesus opens a door, no man can shut it. *"If the Son makes you free, you shall be free indeed"* (John 8:36). So why do millions needlessly languish in the devil's concentration camp? Today is the day of pardon. The Conqueror has crashed through the gates; relief has arrived.

The most famous escape artist of all was Houdini, a show business notable. Police would lock him up in a cell, and as they walked away, he would follow them – already loose within seconds. Except once. Half an hour went by and Houdini still was fuming over the lock. Then a policeman came and simply pushed the door open. The door had never been locked! Houdini was fooled trying to unlock a door that had already been unlocked.

Christ has gone right through the castle of giant despair. He has the keys of death and hell, and He has opened the gates. So why are millions sweating, trying every trick to get out of their bondages? They join new cults or old heathen religions, hear new theories, and go to psychiatrists. But why? Jesus sets men free. He does it all the time. That is the Gospel! You do not preach about it or offer its contents for discussion. The Gospel is not a discussion point. It is a proclamation of deliverance. The Gospel is not open to modification. It is a mandatory, royal, and divine edict. Some systems and theories of deliverance are bondages in themselves, full of lifelong duties and demands. Only Jesus saves! We need to let the world know.

If you are depressed, the worst thing you could do is concentrate on your depression. If you are lonely, the worst thing you can do is focus on your loneliness. And if you are afraid, the worst thing you can do is focus on your fear. Instead of looking inward, begin to look outward to a world that needs a cure for their depression, loneliness and fear – and YOU have the answer! It is not a mere tranquilizer. The Gospel is God's remedy for the problems the world is so acutely aware of in this moment. Don't keep it to yourself! Now is the time to shine!

THE ANOINTING

The Lord's anointed ones are full of active faith! They won't back down to the voice of fear or the appearance of impending destruction.

We read in 1 Samuel 17 the story of David and Goliath. David saw Goliath and heard the blasphemies that came out of his mouth. Eliab listened with a sinking heart. Something different happened to David, though. The anointing of the Lord began to heat up within him. At that same moment, the hearts of Israel's unanointed professionals became ice-cold with fear. Do you see the contrast? This has always been a notable distinction between the two, and it still is today. The anointing gives great boldness, making people immune to fear! The anointing makes the difference between an academic faith and a burning faith. Let me warn you - the one faith will always irritate the other.

Eliab undoubtedly had reason on his side, which left him weighing up the balance of Israelite and Philistine forces. He saw no other resources. Eliab was able to make professional assessments of battle situations, and he saw that Israel had no chance of winning. This professional officer mentally put himself next to Goliath for comparison and saw him as an awesome giant. David, in contrast, was a man of active faith and mentally put Goliath next to the God of Israel and saw the Philistine as a midget. It is amazing what transpires when faith and fear are contrasted.

David knew that he had the Lord on his side, and he felt a holy stirring and indignation within his soul. That was because of the anointing, which gave him resources unknown to others. His inner eyes of faith were upon the Lord. He did more than just hope and pray. God's anointing made him hungry for victory, and he was excited with eager anticipation. The anointing was the "guarantee" of things to come.

Oftentimes, people act in response to a voice of fear that comes disguised as a voice of reason. However, for the anointed believer, it is only reasonable to view every unholy circumstance of opposition as insignificant, compared to our great and mighty God! Rather than allowing the challenging circumstances in your life and in the world around you to paralyze and intimidate you, allow them to stoke the fire in your heart. Allow them to embolden you and stir the anointing on your life.

And you will discover the great resources God has invested into your life and the anointing He has given you.

PICK UP YOUR WEAPONS!

Where are our weapons? Paul wrote, *"Stir up the gift of God which is in you"* (2 Tim. 1:6). He instructed, "Stir up." This word has to do with fire – the stirring up of a campfire to get the embers blazing. It means, "to kindle," "to bring up to full flame." Do not cool off! Stir up that fire! Use the fan on the dying embers. The Word of God and the gifts of the Spirit are our weapons against the attack of the enemy.

These gifts are described in 1 Corinthians 12:1-11; *"Now concerning spiritual gifts, brethren, I do not want you to be unaware. You know that when you were pagans, you were led astray to the mute idols, however you were led. Therefore I make known to you that no one speaking by the Spirit of God says, "Jesus is accursed"; and no one can say, "Jesus is Lord," except by the Holy Spirit. Now there are varieties of gifts, but the same Spirit. And there are varieties of ministries, and the same Lord. There are varieties of effects, but the same God who works all things in all persons. But to each one is given the manifestation of the Spirit for the common good. For to one is given the word of wisdom through the Spirit, and to another the word of knowledge according to the same Spirit; to another faith by the same Spirit, and to another gifts of healing by the one Spirit, and to another the effecting of miracles, and to another prophecy, and to another the distinguishing of spirits, to another various kinds of tongues, and to another the interpretation of tongues. But one and the same Spirit works all these things, distributing to each one individually just as He wills."*

These gifts of the Spirit are our weapons, and the devil has done his best to stop Christians from using them.

As valuable as natural gifts are, they can never take the place of Holy Spirit endued gifts, and more importantly, they must never be confused with them. For example, many churchmen and medical doctors have opposed divine healing. They have magnified the stories of those who are "disappointed" and who are not immediately healed. They have conveniently forgotten that doctors disappoint millions every day. Nearly everyone in the graveyard had been to a doctor first, yet nobody would be so foolish as to demand the closing of all hospitals! Others object to divine healing simply because some are not healed, and so they do not minister to the sick at all. This leaves everybody unhealed! Where is compassion, or obedience to the Scriptures? Some Christians have let their bow and arrows (their gifts, their spiritual weapons) gather dust in a corner because of critics. They lower their God-given weapons and accept defeat because of the fear of man. Others have been hurt, perhaps by remarks from fellow believers, and thus have dropped their gifts. They have "lost" them, though God never reclaims them, for *"the gifts and the calling of God are irrevocable"* (Rom. 11:29).

The Lord has never sent a saint into battle without a weapon. That is precisely why, before His ascension to heaven, Jesus told the apostles to remain in Jerusalem until the coming of the Holy Spirit. He knew that they would need to be endued with the power of the Holy Spirit and His gifts. The power of the Holy Spirit and the spiritual gifts must be recovered to each and every believer.

Hear the word of the Lord:

Go back to the day and to the place where you left those spiritual gifts and ask the Lord to forgive you. Do not be afraid! Do not despair; the gifts are still there, albeit dormant. Dry your tears of despair and sorrow and take up your weapons again!

FEAR IS A PHANTOM!

Do you know, with absolute assurance, that you have joined the winning side?

Then you will not be harassed by fear.

There is no way a believer can be crushed by Satan.

Those who belong to Jesus are unbeatable. You see every Christian has the Winner, Christ Himself, on his side. *"If God is for us, who can be against us?"* (Rom. 8:31). Fear is forged in hell. It is issued by Satan as a standard weapon to all demons. They know the meaning of fear. It has a paralyzing force. Demons are full of fear themselves, as scorpions are full of poison. Fear is Satan's venom. He wants to sting us all, making us sick with fear. The devil will create a future for us packed with frightening images, and roll it out for us, like a reel of film on the screen of our minds. However, they are all illusions. Fears are mere phantoms. They only take on substance if we accept them as truths. We must exorcise these ghosts. Conquering dread is the blow against the enemy that neutralizes his primary attack.

"No weapon formed against you shall prosper" (Isa. 54:17)

We have our own weapon, the sword of the Spirit, which is the Word of God (Eph. 6:17). Know the Word, and learn from it that we are not at the mercy of the devil! You are on the winning side! Satan wants you to believe you are doomed. But that is not so! *"No, in all these things, we are more than conquerors through Him who loved us"* (Romans 8:37). Believe it!

You're more than a conqueror through Jesus!

DRESSED FOR BATTLE

The Bible uses military analogies to describe the way in which followers of Jesus are to prepare for attacks from the devil, whether they come in the form of fear, temptation, iniquity, sickness, or disease.

Paul gives a famous example of this in his letter to the Church in Ephesus, *"A final word: Be strong in the Lord and in his mighty power. Put on all of God's armor so that you will be able to stand firm against all strategies of the devil. For we are not fighting against flesh-and-blood enemies, but against evil rulers and authorities of the unseen world, against mighty powers in this dark world, and against evil spirits in the heavenly places. Therefore, put on every piece of God's armor so you will be able to resist the enemy in the time of evil. Then after the battle you will still be standing firm. Stand your ground, putting on the belt of truth and the body armor of God's righteousness. For shoes, put on the peace that comes from the Good News so that you will be fully prepared. In addition to all of these, hold up the shield of faith to stop the fiery arrows of the devil. Put on salvation as your helmet, and take the sword of the Spirit, which is the word of God. Pray in the Spirit at all times and on every occasion. Stay alert and be persistent in your prayers for all believers everywhere"* (Ephesians 6:10-18).

In ancient times, a soldier in the Roman Empire would put on his complete battle gear before engaging the enemy. Paul explained that in the same manner, we should also be fully dressed in spiritual armor, ready for every battle. Our spiritual armor has both defensive and offensive components designed to protect our spiritual lives. Each piece of this armor serves a specific purpose and provides much needed protection for us.

Salvation, faith, truth, righteousness, and peace are more than Christian virtues – they are components of our spiritual battle gear! We must have these virtues to be both good witnesses for Jesus and effective soldiers in His army. We are God's children of peace; we are likewise His children in war. That means you are destined to face adversity, and destined to win, because God is your Father! Proverbs 24:10 says, *"If you faint in the day of adversity, your strength is small."* We put on salvation, faith, truth, and righteousness, so we can stand strong against the devil's weapons formed against us.

There is another weapon in our arsenal that packs the biggest punch to the kingdom of darkness! It's the ultimate spiritual weapon known to mankind, and the only force strong enough to render Satan a defeated foe now and forevermore! Have you guessed what it is already? It's the precious blood of Jesus! The cross was the ultimate thermonuclear bomb to the armies of hell. The poured-out blood of Jesus forever changed the trajectory of every battle that ever was and ever will be, to a complete triumph over the kingdom of darkness! Jesus has already won the victory over hell and death! It is up to us to believe it and align ourselves with this truth! *"And they overcame him by the blood of the Lamb and by the word of their testimony, and they did not love their lives to the death"* (Revelation 12:11). The only ones that have any reason to fear are those who are fighting in futility on the dark side! However, we stand dressed and ready for every battle, knowing we have already been declared overcomers through the powerful blood of Jesus!

THE SAFEST PLACE ON EARTH — "IN CHRIST"

The opposite of fear is faith. But what is true faith? Wholeheartedly trusting Christ Jesus is real faith. We trust Christ in a way that is deeper than our trust in anything or anyone else. It means surrender, letting Him take over – not just in one area of our lives, but over our entire lives.

Peter showed this kind of faith when he stepped out of the boat to walk on water to the Lord (Matthew 14:22-33). Sometimes Peter gets a bad rap for allowing the fear of the waves to shake his resolve, but the rest of the disciples didn't even attempt to step out of the boat! But Peter had faith in who Jesus was and because of that relationship, he dared to leap! But when he took his eyes off of the Lord, and saw the wind and the waves coming towards him, he became afraid and cried out, "Lord, save me!" Immediately, Jesus reached out His hand to Peter and caught him.

If the Lord is going to keep your head above water, He has to get a grip on you completely. That's what Paul desired for his new converts to Christ. *"Now may the God of peace Himself sanctify you completely; and may your whole spirit, soul, and body be preserved blameless at the coming of our Lord Jesus Christ"* (1 Thessalonians 5:23).

Jesus can only save what we give to Him. We must hand everything over to Him – lock, stock, and barrel; body, soul, and spirit – giving ourselves into His total care for all time. It's total trust in Who He is. You see, believing is a relationship. I do not mean like being related to your great-aunt Betsy, whom you've never met. Our relationship with Jesus is both alive and thriving! We give ourselves to Him, and He gives Himself to us. We become *"partakers of the divine nature"* (2 Peter 1:4).

The apostle Paul uses a marvelous expression to describe this relationship – "in Christ." For example, *"if anyone is in Christ, he is a new creation"* (2 Corinthians 5:17), and *"there is therefore now no condemnation to those who are in Christ Jesus"* (Romans 8:1). The simplest faith in Christ has this amazing effect. All true faith is simple anyway. Even a child can grasp it! It is not some kind of algebra to find the value of X. The simplest person can believe and enjoy the same effect as the wisest. Jesus heard all the religious jargon of the scribes, which ordinary people did not appreciate. But the common people heard Jesus gladly. He talked about faith, but put it in other ways.

"Come to Me."
"Love Me."
"Abide in Me."
"Follow Me."

Faith is not one particular religious act. It is the transfer of responsibility for our lives to God in total when our own resources are inadequate. Faith is spiritual fusion, making us one in Christ!

GOD'S PLAN FOR YOUR HEALTH

We often take good health for granted – until something threatens it! Unfortunately, so many people experience sickness and disease, which was never God's idea. The Gospel of Jesus Christ is God's national health plan for every nation on earth, and the Bible is its textbook. Somebody said that God meant our bodies to last, with care, for a lifetime! The first page of the Bible says, *"God saw everything that He had made, and indeed it was very good"* (Genesis 1:31). The last page says, *"There shall be no more death, nor sorrow, nor crying... no more pain"* (Revelation 21:4). Things began very well and they will end that way.

The Lord's plan for you since the beginning of time is for you to *"prosper and be in health, even as your soul prospers"* (3 John 1:2). Sickness in God's good world is like weeds growing among wheat. But make no mistake – God did not sow the weeds. *"An enemy did this"* (Matthew 13:28). The Father sent Jesus who *"went about healing all who were oppressed by the devil, for God was with Him"* (Acts 10:38). It was the Creator's protest against the sabotage of His work by the devil. *"The thief comes only to steal and kill and destroy; I came that they may have life, and have it abundantly"* (John 10:10).

God planned cures in nature which medical research keeps finding. But the God who heals naturally, also heals supernaturally! The Bible makes it clear that sickness is not God's will, and in contrast, it credits all healings to God. Today, His hand touches far more people than many even realize. Throughout the world, many supernatural healings take place every year, proving that *"Jesus Christ is the same yesterday, today, and forever"* (Hebrews 13:8).

It has been said that the Bible holds, not only the "words" of God, but also the "Word" of God – His solemn and heart-felt promises. And while He didn't have to make a written legal agreement with mankind, nonetheless, when He gave us His "Word," He memorialized those promises in writing. Interestingly, both terms for the old and new sections of our Bible, "covenant" and "testament," are legal terms, which in this case refer to a binding agreement between the King of kings, who governs the universe, and mankind, His creation. Legally binding or not, when God gives His Word, you can count on it, it is unbreakable. He means what He says and says what He means! And whatever your position on the covenant of healing may be, there is no challenging the reality that it is both a biblical promise and a mandate for His people.

In the wisdom, love, and tender mercies of God, He reaches out to heal the whole person – those with broken hearts as well as those with broken bodies.

Be encouraged! When God gives His Word and makes a promise... you can believe Him. You have nothing to fear because His plans for you are for good! *"For I know the plans I have for you," declares the Lord, "plans to prosper you and not to harm you, plans to give you hope and a future"* (Jeremiah 29:11).

THE FAITH OF ABRAHAM

The Bible names Abraham 309 times, but because of his faith, his name is inscribed upon the whole of the Middle East and upon world history to this day. We can learn a lot about Abraham from the book of Genesis.

"Some time later, the Lord spoke to Abram in a vision and said to him, 'Do not be afraid, Abram, for I will protect you, and your reward will be great.' But Abram replied, 'O Sovereign Lord, what good are all your blessings when I don't even have a son? Since you've given me no children, Eliezer of Damascus, a servant in my household, will inherit all my wealth. You have given me no descendants of my own, so one of my servants will be my heir.' Then the Lord said to him, 'No, your servant will not be your heir, for you will have a son of your own who will be your heir.' Then the Lord took Abram outside and

said to him, 'Look up into the sky and count the stars if you can. That's how many descendants you will have!' And Abram believed the Lord, and the Lord counted him as righteous because of his faith." (Genesis 15:1-6)

Abraham was the first person recognized for the "obedience of faith," as his life consistently lined up with his faith in God. *"Abraham believed God, and it was accounted to him for righteousness"* (Romans 4:3). Fears are volatile, but what is of faith lasts forever!

Remember this: fears die with the fearful, but those who are full of faith forever change the world!

Abraham was a world changer! In fact, he is responsible for beginning the civilizing process fifteen hundred years before the Greeks and Romans. The Pharaohs were in Egypt one thousand years before Abraham, and continued another two thousand years after he died, but they did not affect the world as much as he did. The Pharaohs left no moral mark, and only cluttered the desert sands with colossal monuments to their own egos. Abraham did not leave a single commemorative ornament behind for us to see, but all our lives today – religious or not – are impacted by his life.

Abraham was not deeply religious. He was not even religious in our modern sense. He had no creed, no hymns, no Bible, no images, and no theology. He probably did not really know much about God, but he *knew* God personally and very well. When it comes to faith, a personal relationship with the Lord is all that matters! Abraham walked with God and was a friend of God. For this patriarch, God was not a Sunday morning service obligation. He had no church to attend. Abraham did not believe God just to be faithful to some sort of tradition. There was no tradition. God was his way of life because God was real to him!

God revealed Himself to Abraham and gave him a simple instruction – to leave Ur. God didn't tell Abraham where to go. Nevertheless, Abraham set off. This began his unforgettable life of faith. Hebrews 11:8-10 describes it:

"By faith Abraham obeyed when he was called to go out to the place which he would receive as an inheritance. And he went out, not knowing where he was going. By faith he dwelt in the land of promise as in a foreign country, dwelling in tents with Isaac and Jacob, the heirs with him of the same promise; for he waited for the city which has foundations, whose builder and maker is God."

God had promised Abraham he would be the first of a great nation whose God is the Lord. God said: *"I will make you a great nation; I will bless you and make your name great; and you shall be a blessing. I will bless those who bless you, and I will curse him who curses you; and in you all the families of the earth shall be blessed."* (Genesis 12:2-3) It's important to note, that when Isaac – the first seed of this promise – finally came, the Lord told Abraham to sacrifice him on the altar! To be willing (right or wrong) to sacrifice Isaac showed astounding trust in the Lord!

As we read in Hebrews, Abraham believed God could raise Isaac from the dead if necessary. But the voice of God, at the most dramatic moment, stopped Abraham's hand from slaying his son. Abraham had passed the ultimate test of his faith! He exhibited incredible faith, because he fully trusted the Lord and expected Isaac would be the father of generations and nations, simply because the Lord had said so.

Abraham didn't doubt the Lord. Therefore, the Lord didn't doubt Abraham! In fact, God was so pleased with him, He took Abraham's name as part of His own name! He called Himself, "The God of Abraham". The Almighty identified Himself with a man. This means God's reputation rested on Abraham. What God was like – a new God to the world in general – would be assumed from what Abraham was like. God risked His name by joining it with Abraham.

Abraham believed in the Lord, and the Lord believed in Abraham! Something similar is reflected in what Jesus said in Matthew 10:32, *"Whoever confesses Me before men, him I will also confess before My Father who is in heaven."* This is the deepest truth about faith. Its primary purpose is not merely getting things or doing things or being something. It relates us to God. Faith is fellowship, and it is always the condition for our relationship with God. He puts faith in our hearts, and then He puts His faith in us to do His will.

John 2:23-24 says, *"Many believed in His name...but Jesus did not commit Himself to them, because He knew all men."* The words "commit Himself" are the same as believe. Their faith was not right, and Jesus knew it.

But when faith is right, Jesus does commit Himself to us! Imagine that! Christ comes to us in trust!

The whole business of God's promises, dealings, association, and relations with us becomes possible once this mutual trust is established. God transmitted who He was to Abraham through his faith, and He will do the same for us if we only believe!

YOU ARE IMMUNE TO THE CURSE!

Fear plays into the hands of the devil. The truth is, he can do no real damage, except to make us fear that he can. The devil is a con artist. Try as he may to stop the people of God with his wicked schemes, he is forever a failure because we are forever covered by the blood of the lamb!

The story of Balak's plot to curse Israel in Numbers 22-24 shows us this example. Up until this point, Israel had been undefeated on the battlefield. Balak, the king of Moab, was determined to change Israel's winning streak. He desired to rid the land of God's people, so he resorted to other means to come against them. He offered Balaam, the prophet, money to put a curse on Israel. Unfortunately, Balaam was willing because he loved money. He knew that the Lord did not want to curse Israel, but he asked anyway, just in case. He sought the Lord, hoping that God would give him that kind of a prophecy.

Balak and Balaam clambered up to the rocky peaks of "the high places of Baal" and built seven altars. There they offered seven bulls and seven rams in sacrifice, hoping that some dark, occult force might oblige them and hinder the progress of God's people. However, God does not deal in curses against His own people! Yet Balaam and Balak persisted, trying hard from every angle, but they found the attempt was utterly futile. They looked at the tents of Israel at the foot of the high hills. In the midst of the camp was the tabernacle, with the cloud of God's presence, the very banner of the Lord, constantly there. *"He who keeps Israel shall neither slumber nor sleep"* (Psalms 121:4). Early in the morning, Israel was resting, safe beneath the outspread wings of Jehovah, which were invisible to Israel's enemies.

Balaam was forced to speak the truth and speak a blessing over Israel. He showed us that God's people are not for cursing. We are immune. We are redeemed, as was Israel. What was true of God's redeemed people then, is true of the redeemed today! Fear hears the shout of the enemy, but faith hears the shout of the King of kings. *"There is no sorcery against Jacob, nor any divination against Israel. It now must be said of Jacob and of Israel, 'Oh, what God has done!'"* (Numbers 23:23).

Incidentally, this verse reminds me of the many times that witch doctors have attempted to curse our Gospel campaigns. Many times, the proclamation of a simple but anointed "Hallelujah!" from the platform has broken the yoke of oppression and sent witches wheezing and choking for breath! Their attempts to curse us and call up demons have been foiled by God's mighty protection. Truly, *"The angel of the LORD encamps all around those who fear Him"* (Psalms 34:7).

When the howling winds of death were heard across Egypt at the Passover, no Israeli home knew its cold breath. When the Lord passed through Egypt smiting all the firstborn in the land, He passed over all the houses on which He saw the blood of the lamb.

"On that night I will pass through the land of Egypt and strike down every firstborn son and firstborn male animal in the land of Egypt. I will execute judgment against all the gods of Egypt, for I am the Lord! But the blood on your doorposts will serve as a sign, marking the houses where you are staying. When I see the blood, I will pass over you. This plague of death will not touch you when I strike the land of Egypt." (Exodus 12:12-13)

Every child of God today is covered and marked by the blood of Jesus. Each one of us is beyond the reach of the powers of hell, witches, spells, curses, demons, or all the devil's minions. The principalities and powers in heavenly places cannot touch us while we rest beneath the banner of the precious blood of our Savior, our Passover Lamb. His protection surrounding us is impenetrable and invulnerable. Psalm 121:5-8 describes the Lord's protective banner over us, *"The Lord himself watches over you! The Lord stands beside you as your protective shade. The sun will not harm you by day, nor the moon at night. The Lord keeps you from all harm and watches over your life. The Lord keeps watch over you as you come and go, both now and forever."*

STAY FOCUSED

Wherever your heart, eyes, and mind are set, is where the rest of you will end up eventually. We become whatever we behold. There was an article in the *New York Times* called, "Long-Married Couples Do Look Alike, Study Finds." In this article Dr. Zajonc, a psychologist at the University of Michigan, proposed that "people, often unconsciously, mimic the facial expressions of their spouses in a silent empathy and that, over the years, sharing the same expressions shapes the face similarly." Modern Science has finally discovered a biblical revelation from long ago – you become whatever you behold. *"But we all, with unveiled face, beholding as in a mirror the glory of the Lord, are being transformed into the same image from glory to glory, just as by the Spirit of the Lord"* (2 Corinthians 3:18). What we set our attention on, with our eyes, minds, and hearts, has this incredible ability to transform us from the inside out!

When I was a young boy, my father taught me how to mow our lawn. He instructed me to set my eyes on a target straight ahead at the other end of the yard and aim for it. That way, I would end up going straight towards my focal point, and my lawn stripes would be straight as a result. Whatever you focus on, whatever you give your attention to, will grow in your life. Ultimately, what you give your attention to will influence you one way or another. If you are focused on only the bad news you hear (i.e. darkness, demonic activity, and negative thinking in general) you will undoubtedly find yourself in more and more bondage. You will see demons in every corner, even when they aren't there.

One of Satan's most powerful weapons is fear. Hebrews 2:15 tells us that fear can bring bondage. *"Inasmuch then as the children have partaken of flesh and blood, He Himself likewise shared in the same, that through death He might destroy him who had the power of death, that is, the devil, and release those who through fear of death were all their lifetime subject to bondage."*

Satan wants you to be so distracted by what he is doing in the world, that you forget what you are supposed to be doing in the world! He wants you to forget that you are a born-again victor over the kingdom of darkness! You see, fear paralyzes people from walking out the call of God on their lives. The devil thrives on fear, and evil depends on it.

The antidote to fear is love, which comes from God of course! Paul explains it perfectly, *"For God has not given us a spirit of fear, but of power and of love and of a sound mind"* (2 Timothy 1:7). If you are focused on darkness, then fear will rule your life. If you focus on God, then love will rule your heart. First John 4:18 tells us, "There is no fear in love. But perfect love drives out fear, because fear has to do with punishment. The one who fears is not made perfect in love."

As Smith Wigglesworth said,

"If you have a great God, you will have a little devil; if you have a big devil, you will have a little God."

To keep the right perspective, we must keep our attention on Jesus, the author and perfecter of our faith!

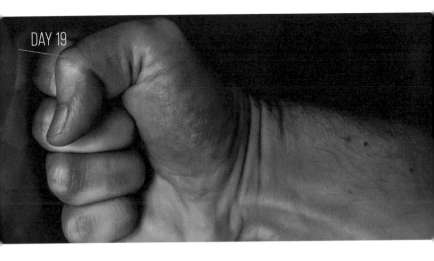

YOU HAVE THE SUPERIOR FORCE!

The man who lives in fear is the devil's ally – whether he likes it or not. The fearful help Satan accomplish his plans in the earth. Fear is an infection, a sickness of the soul. Unfortunately, it can spread among Christians. I am sure the reason why God prohibited the children of Israel from talking while marching around the walls of Jericho was that they would have spread doubt and fear among themselves.

"Now Joshua had commanded the people, saying, "You shall not shout or make any noise with your voice, nor shall a word proceed out of your mouth, until the day I say to you, 'Shout!' Then you shall shout." (Joshua 6:10)

The devil does not fear the man who fears. He knows that person is harmless. However, Satan trembles when we do *not* fear! When Nehemiah was restoring Jerusalem, he was urged to hide from his enemies. I like his reply: *"Should such a man as I flee? And who is there such as I who would go into the temple to save his life? I will not go in!"* (Nehemiah 6:11). Are the people of God, the blood-bought sons and daughters of the kingdom, to give way to bluster and threats? God's people are not given *"a spirit of fear, but of power and of love and of a sound mind"* (2 Timothy 1:7).

Far from fearing, we can rejoice! *"Behold, I give you the authority to trample on serpents and scorpions, and over all the power of the enemy, and nothing shall by any means hurt you"* (Luke 10:19).

Christians are not the hunted but the hunters – not the attacked but the attackers! We are not the surrounded. We do not have our backs up against a wall. Far from it!

We are God's elite troops, sent to release the hostages of hell!

We are the invading forces of the Lord!

Repeatedly, Jesus told us, *"Fear not!"* However, that was not all that He said. He was the supreme psychologist. Notice what He said: *"Do not be afraid, only believe"* (Luke 8:50). It was always more than just, "Hey you, chin up!" "Don't be afraid," or "Take courage, be brave." That alone would be useless advice. Fear is a force, and it must be met by a superior force! Fear is the negative force. Its sign is a minus. Somebody once said to me, "Fear is the darkroom in which people develop their negatives." Only a positive force can cancel a negative one. That positive force is faith in Jesus! Jesus is saying to you today, *"Do not be afraid; only believe."*

The opposite of fear is not courage, but faith! *"This is the victory that has overcome the world – our faith"* (1 John 5:4). We must realize, we are not only those who overcome fear – we are those who turn the tables on Satan and send the armies of hell running away in fear instead! We create terror and chaos in the enemy's camp when we move and act upon the word of God in faith!

THE ANT AND THE ELEPHANT

God's children should be bold. Take the parents of Moses for example, *"By faith Moses, when he was born, was hidden three months by his parents, because they saw he was a beautiful child; and they were not afraid of the king's command"* (Hebrews 11:23).

Just think of what that involved. The Egyptian state, with Pharaoh at its head, had made it illegal to keep a male Hebrew baby. By law, such children were to be killed at birth. The panic and horror of the Hebrews must have been palpable as soldiers moved around the city to carry out this murderous order. What terror and grief there must have been!

Then Moses was born. His parents looked upon their lovely son, and they knew they could not, and never would, allow him to be killed. They decided to defy the law and hide the baby. *"By faith … they were not afraid."* Officers of the law were around, and their footsteps were heard stopping at their very door, seeking the child's life! Who would not shake in their shoes if armed men were waiting, ready to kill their baby? Yet "they were not afraid." Why not? Were they unnatural, unfeeling? No, they were very good parents. There was just one reason why they did not quiver or panic – they had faith in the Almighty God! True, the situation was impossible. Their faith looked naive and foolish. Nevertheless, the situation was exactly what God likes: *"For with God nothing will be impossible"* (Luke 1:37).

When things are impossible, faith is the answer. Faith is not just for the possible – that is not faith at all. The mightiest resource in the universe is the arm of God. Some can only believe God when it is for something "reasonable," something that can be managed. However, Paul wrote, *"We … have no confidence in the flesh"* (Philippians 3:3), that is, in our own schemes.

I love to illustrate faith in a big God with the delightful African story of the elephant and the ant. An elephant crossed a shaky bridge, and a tiny ant sat on the elephant, just behind the huge animal's ear. The bridge shook as they crossed, and when they were safely on the other side, the ant said to the elephant, "My word! We made that bridge swing all right, didn't we?" This is the relationship we have with God when we rest on Him. He carries us!

"For from days of old they have not heard or perceived by ear, nor has the eye seen a God besides You, Who acts in behalf of the one who waits for Him" (Isaiah 46:4).

He makes the bridge swing.
He puts His weight behind us and on our side.
He builds your home, your church, and your business.
He heals you;
He guides you;
He protects you;
He carries you!

The Lord always leads you to triumph! In Him, we find the impossible possible. Hallelujah!

GOD IS NOT IN HIDING

Some people believe that God has distanced Himself from
mankind. They view Him as being withdrawn, uninvolved, and
even apathetic towards His creation. But since Jesus came,
the Father God has revealed Himself more and more! He
manifested Himself through His Son Jesus and then sent His
Holy Spirit to be with us for always. Jesus said, *"Have I been
with you all this time, Philip, and yet you still don't know who
I am? Anyone who has seen me has seen the Father! So why are
you asking me to show him to you?"* (John 14:9).

His presence and power are vivid in the Bible and in the world,
even to this very day. If anybody thinks God has dwindled away
or disappeared, let him or her come to Africa! I have seen Him
there, manifested in greater power than anywhere in the Old
Testament. I have seen Him expelling demons, restoring the

sick, and healing the blind, the cripples, and the deaf. God did not do that even with Moses! God is shaking cities and nations. Perhaps that is where God "disappeared to" – living among those who believe Him!

The idea that God disappeared is an old fear of unbelief. Israel participated in the Exodus, saw His glory, and knew it was all true. But within months, they became mistrustful and afraid. They wanted something to see, so they made a golden calf to lead them back into slavery (see Exodus 32). Unbelief always leads to slavery, but faith leads to freedom! However, the Israelites lost all of their passports and visas of faith in God and never crossed the border into the Promised Land, with two exceptions – Caleb and Joshua, who held onto their faith and entered in.

Unbelief is that ancient. It is neither clever nor modern. We can trace it all the way back to the Garden of Eden, where Eve doubted. For her and us, doubt is a satanic piece of foolishness that never did anybody any good. If we are to relate to God, how on earth can we do it except by trusting Him? He will not have much trust with those who give Him the cold shoulder or pretend He does not exist. He owes us nothing, and if we want it to be that way, He will not interfere.

"And even as they did not like to retain God in their knowledge, God gave them over to a debased mind, to do those things which are not fitting" (Romans 1:28).

Jesus is alive and well and moving in the earth! You know, there are some who have never even seen a miracle with their own two eyes, yet they exhibit the most faith! Very few people ever saw a miracle until Christ came. Still, there were men and women before His time who displayed amazing faith! Jesus spoke of them and said,

"Blessed are those who have not seen and yet have believed" (John 20:29).

They read the Scriptures and believed the God of the Exodus could not fail them and would work on their behalf. And He did! David, for example, never saw a miracle and had only the slightest experience of the supernatural, yet he forged ahead in total expectation of divine help – and He got it! Today, three thousand years later, his faith is still a model for us. Maybe you can relate to David. Maybe you have not seen the miraculous with your own two eyes and yet you know it takes place, and you know God is able, simply because you believe His Word is true! If that's you, know this; your faith is known by heaven, and the Lord calls you "blessed!"

STAND ON THE SOLID ROCK

We are commonly told today to keep an open mind about our beliefs and how we interpret the Word of God. We are told to never be dogmatic. Some have no problem cherry-picking the scriptures or changing the meaning or validity of it all together! There has been a practice of using the Word of God only when it's agreeable or relatable to the listening audience. This is totally perverted! It's a liberal view that means, "you can never be sure," and worse, "if you don't like it, you can change it." What use is the Word of God if it can be changed? What use is faith in the truth if truth is variable?

The Word of God is meant to assure us about both God and our future. If we keep an open mind about it, we brush aside all of Christ's wonderful promises and enjoy nothing at all of what He guarantees. True Christians do not keep an open mind. Keeping an open mind regarding God or His Word is just an excuse for sin and unbelief. Christians embrace the entire Word of God! We embrace the positive blessings of Christ. Our minds are settled, not open!

Some people act as if believing nothing for sure is a virtue! It certainly is not a virtue in an airplane pilot! How many would board an aircraft if the pilot decided to keep an open mind about how to fly, the destination, and how to get there? Passengers want a very dogmatic pilot! He must be certain they will not end up dead! Keeping an open mind about our journey through life is equally perilous. What is our destination? We must know!

The Bible does not encourage anybody to be dogmatic, but its language is always that of a sure and certain hope. "We know" is a typical New Testament expression. Being sure is not being presumptuous or arrogant. Being sure that the sun will rise tomorrow makes us neither dogmatic nor overconfident. And such surety is the simple attitude of Christians, who are confident of tomorrow and of God. What He has done, He will do, and what He is, He will be!

The common Christian testimony is that of the apostle Paul: *"I know whom I have believed and am persuaded that He is able to keep what I have committed to Him until that Day"* (2 Timothy 1:12), or the day when Christ comes. That kind of certainty is no more than we would expect from any God worth calling God! An open mind is a mind susceptible to the attack of the enemy. An open mind is an open door to doubt, fear, and unbelief. We are to have a sound mind! *"For God has not given us a spirit of fear, but of power, and of love, and of a sound mind"* (2 Timothy 1:7).

Our belief in Christ is our sure foundation! Jesus is a solid rock to stand on! He is the peace of a settled mind fixed on Him. He is the anchor of hope for the blood-bought soul! He is the everlasting rock for those who fear Him! And those who put their trust in Him will not be shaken! Psalm 18:2 says, *"The Lord is my rock, my fortress and my deliverer; my God is my rock, in whom I take refuge, my shield and the horn of my salvation, my stronghold."*

There's nothing wishy-washy about Jesus or His word. We must trust in the Lord wholeheartedly without any doubt, *"for the one who doubts is like the surf of the sea, driven and tossed by the wind. For that man ought not to expect that He will receive anything from the Lord, being a double-minded man, unstable in all his ways"* (James 1:6-8).

We can choose to have a settled mind!
We can choose to take every thought captive to obey Christ! (2 Corinthians 10:5.)

We can stand unwavering on the word of God, because God Himself backs it up!

GOD'S PROMISES ARE RELIABLE

"Not one of the good promises which the Lord had made to the house of Israel failed; all came to pass." (Joshua 21:45)

Faith is a personal issue.

Somebody may have proven himself or herself up to now, but the future holds only personal assurances. We trust certain people because we know them personally. If we thought these people would change, we would not trust them. We read in the Bible who God is, and we may have proven Him for ourselves in our own lives, yet for the future, we still must trust Him.

No faith is needed to believe two plus two makes four, but life is a degree more complicated than basic math. Circumstances change like the ocean. The vast variables of all things affect their outcome. However, God is all-wise and all-powerful, so much so, that we have to leave things to Him to sort out, because ultimately, He holds the future. We may not understand all that He is doing, but we look to Him in trust, and that is something God takes into account. He made the world that way. There is no doubt that God can do anything, but He does not work apart from those who believe. Prayer and faith will enable Him to do what He could not do otherwise, because He is sovereign and just. You see, He designed prayer and faith to go hand in hand – this is His planned providence.

It is human nature to depend on people's promises until we are disillusioned. Tricksters and conmen depend on this innate trust in people who give us their word. We should be able to trust the Almighty God! Not only has He given us His Word, a hundred generations have proven Him to be reliable! *"Jesus Christ is the same yesterday, today, and forever"* (Hebrews 13:8).

He has given us all the same reason for relying on Him – expressed declarations of what He will do for us. Somebody went through the whole Bible and found at total of 7,874 promises that God had made to us. That glittering array of promises covers our understanding of God and what we can expect of Him. The scope of 7,874 promises should be wide enough for all the circumstances in our lives in need of God's help. Many of God's promises come in the form of a covenant. God does a lot for us without us needing to ask Him.

"Your Father in heaven...makes His sun rise on the evil and on the good, and sends rain on the just and on the unjust" (Matthew 5:45).

God is good, and good to all. Millions give Him no credit, though they are quick to blame Him when things go wrong. The processes of nature seem unchangeable and regular. To this day, nobody has shown that God has no part in this. He keeps His promises to *"the birds, the cattle, and every beast of the earth"* (Genesis 9:10). *"While the earth remains, seedtime and harvest, cold and heat, winter and summer, and day and night shall not cease"* (Genesis 8:22).

Jesus took it farther and included the flowers, saying,

"Consider the lilies of the field, how they grow: they neither toil nor spin; and yet I say to you that even Solomon in all his glory was not arrayed like one of these" (Matthew 6:28-29).

However, God has other good things. The promise is, "Seek and you will find" (Matthew 7:7), for they are obtainable only by direct application. Actually, they are promised, and most of them are listed in Scripture – *"No good thing will He withhold from those who walk uprightly"* (Psalm 84:11). When we come to the end of natural provision, Jesus said, *"Ask and you will receive"* (John 16:24). *"Everyone who asks receives... If you then, being evil, know how to give good gifts to your children, how much more will your Father who is in heaven give good things to those who ask Him"* (Matthew 7:8,11).

If we ask for good, He will not send evil – ever!

"Every good gift and every perfect gift is from above, and comes down from the Father of lights" (James 1:17).

The exercise of faith in prayer is paramount! The bird in the nest must learn to fly and gather what is available. Having to ask is an excellent reminder to us of our dependency on God, and prayer is designed to bring us to seek Him. It gives birth to a spirit of childlikeness, causing us to look to our heavenly Father at all times. It is fellowship – family fellowship with our Father. And Glory to God! He has proven Himself to be a *good* Father whose promises never fail!

ANCHORED BY HOPE

Due to the COVID-19 crisis, in just a short span of time, the entire world had to adjust to a new lifestyle of being quarantined. Everyone has been affected by the changes in our societies. We have experienced event cancelations, restaurant and business closings, school closings, mandatory absences from the workplace, and adjusting to "attending" church online at home in our pajamas.

We discovered many new inconveniences, but we also discovered that we can live without a lot of things! The luxuries that our lives sometimes revolve around may often inadvertently be regarded as vital, but the truth is, it's not a matter of life or death if we don't go out to dinner, see the latest blockbuster movie, or spring for that epic new jacket – it won't make or break us. Even necessities like food and water can be sidestepped under the right circumstances – a case in point is fasting, either for health considerations or biblical pursuits.

However, there is one thing we cannot live without under any circumstance… hope! Hope is so fundamentally vital to our inner man, that if we cannot find true hope, we will default by nature to grasp on to false hope. To hope is to be human. God has woven the need to hope in Him into the tapestry of our hearts. And because we are hard-wired to hope in this way, those who don't know God will revere something they perceive as greater than themselves and place their hope in it. It may be money, a dream, prestige, or even another person, but as sure as the night is dark, we will find something to hope in. Yet, in God's deep abiding love, He longs for us to hope in Him as any other hope is built on a lie that will deceive and ultimately betray our trust in it.

In His Word, the Lord chronicles the vast extent of the hope He has brought into our relationship with Him, from His mercy to His coming. There are many Scripture passages that express the heart of God in the many ways He yearns for us to hope in Him.

We hope in His mercy:

"My soul still remembers and sinks within me. This I recall to my mind, therefore I have hope. Through the Lord's mercies we are not consumed, because His compassions fail not. They are new every morning; great is Your faithfulness. "The Lord is my portion," says my soul, "Therefore I hope in Him!"
(Lamentations 3:20-24)

"Behold, the eye of the Lord is on those who fear Him, on those who hope in His mercy." (Psalms 33:18)

"Let Your mercy, O Lord, be upon us, just as we hope in You." (Psalms 33:22)

"But I have trusted in Your mercy; my heart shall rejoice in Your salvation." (Psalms 13:5)

We hope in His Word:

"Those who fear You will be glad when they see me, because I have hoped in Your word." (Psalms 119:74)

"Uphold me according to Your word, that I may live; and do not let me be ashamed of my hope." (Psalms 119:116)

"But Jesus answered him, saying, "It is written, 'Man shall not live by bread alone, but by every word of God.'" (Matthew 4:4)

"You are my hiding place and my shield; I hope in Your word." (Psalms 119:114)

We hope in His unfailing love:

"The Lord your God in your midst, The Mighty One, will save; He will rejoice over you with gladness, He will quiet you with His love, He will rejoice over you with singing." (Zephaniah 3:17)

"For God so loved the world that He gave His only begotten Son, that whoever believes in Him should not perish but have everlasting life." (John 3:16)

"As the Father loved Me, I also have loved you; abide in My love. If you keep My commandments, you will abide in My love, just as I have kept My Father's commandments and abide in His love." (John 15:9-10)

"But God demonstrates His own love toward us, in that while we were still sinners, Christ died for us." (Romans 5:8)

I pray you are encouraged and strengthened by these promises from God's word today. These are just a few – there are thousands more! We believe, in the midst of uncertain times, that we can remain anchored in His love, anchored in His Word, and anchored in Him.

We can rest in the knowledge that hope in His promises will never let us down, and always lift us up, bringing us even closer to Him.

THE TESTING OF YOUR FAITH

The Scripture tells us that the testing and trial of our faith will come, and it also tells us why. 1 Peter 1:7 says, *"So that the tested genuineness of your faith – more precious than gold that perishes though it is tested by fire – may be found to result in praise and glory and honor at the revelation of Jesus Christ."*

I remember when the testing of my faith came. I was sitting on the side of my bed in Malawi. I had a three-dollar-per-day room in a Baptist hostel. I had to sit down because a shock had just hit me. An urgent phone call from my office in Frankfurt, Germany, had brought me news that I could not take in. We were hundreds of thousands of dollars in the red! How could that be? At the beginning of that year, the Lord had assured me it would be "a year of twelve full baskets, a basket for each month." I could not see how we could be in debt. "Lord," I said, "why? You said that there would be full baskets, but they are all empty. How can that be?" In such moments, the Lord opens our eyes. He instructed me by saying, "The baskets of the disciples started filling only after the multitudes had all eaten. Keep on feeding the multitudes with My Word, and I will see to filling up the baskets." I was amazed. The divine wisdom made sense. I said, "Lord, I will do what You say, and I know You will do what You say." But – hundreds of thousands of dollars! It seemed beyond reason. Yes, but God reasons differently. The baskets stayed empty for twenty-four hours, and then came the news that God had filled them again. The year ended without debt. We kept on feeding the multitudes with the Word of God, and the Lord kept handing the supplies to us. When we are breaking the Bread of Life to the spiritually starving, God cannot let us down.

That year, we saw one and a half million precious people respond to the call of God to be saved in our African campaigns alone. Each of us, no matter the manner in which we have been called to serve the Lord, will have our faith tested – and most certainly more than once! Jesus spoke to his own disciples about the testing of their faith that would come.

Luke 22:31-32 says, *"Simon, Simon, behold, Satan demanded to have you, that he might sift you like wheat, but I have prayed for you that your faith may not fail. And when you have turned again, strengthen your brothers."*

Jesus knew that Simon Peter was about to face a greater trial and test of his faith than ever before. This trial of faith that was still to come would be bigger than the storm they had faced on the sea. This test would prove more difficult than their instruction to feed the multitudes with only a basket of food. This test would be more challenging for Simon Peter than stepping out of the boat to walk on water with the Lord. However, Jesus had prayed for Simon, that his faith would not fail, and that when he turned, he would be able to strengthen those around him. Jesus prayed for him, that his faith would not fail. Jesus is praying that our faith will not fail! We must hold on to our faith!

In every season, in every trial, in every circumstance, Jesus is interceding for His church – that we would keep trusting Him, keep standing on His word, and keep looking up!

"I lift up my eyes to the hills. From where does my help come? My help comes from the Lord, who made heaven and earth." (Psalm 121:1-2)

When we face trials of various kinds, when our faith is being tested by fire – we keep looking up and keep our eyes fixed on Jesus! We hold fast to our faith, believing our help comes from the Lord! We will make it through this trial to the other side even stronger than before, and we will go forward encouraging the rest of the saints!

DO NOT BE AFRAID; ONLY BELIEVE

The Lord moves in action on our behalf when we pray and believe!

"So, Jesus answered and said to them, "Have faith in God. For assuredly, I say to you, whoever says to this mountain, 'Be removed and be cast into the sea,' and does not doubt in his heart, but believes that those things he says will be done, he will have whatever he says. Therefore, I say to you, whatever things you ask when you pray, believe that you receive them, and you will have them." (Mark 11:22-24)

It is the Lord's good pleasure to do for us what we ask when we step out in faith! Faith is pleasing to God and it gets His attention. When our attention is on Him, His attention is on us. When we seek to please Him, He seeks to please us, and grant us what we ask.

"But without faith it is impossible to please Him, for he who comes to God must believe that He is, and that He is a rewarder of those who diligently seek Him." (Hebrews 11:6)

Our faith in Christ identifies us as being those on the winning team! He has overcome the world, so that all those who have been won into the Kingdom have, in the same token, won victory over the world! *"For whatever is born of God overcomes the world. And this is the victory that has overcome the world - our faith"* (1 John 5:4). Hebrews 11:1 says, *"Now faith is the substance of things hoped for, the evidence of things not seen."*

Mark, chapter five, gives an account of two people who acted in faith despite the devastating circumstances they were experiencing. Jairus had just implored the Lord to come heal his daughter, who was at the point of death, when the woman with the issue of blood reached out and touched the Lord. The Bible says that she believed that even if she could only touch the garment Jesus was wearing, she would be healed! What incredible faith! Jesus immediately stopped and asked who had touched Him. When he learned of her story, He told her, "Your faith has made you well..." *"While He was still speaking, some came from the ruler of the synagogue's house who said, "Your daughter is dead. Why trouble the Teacher any further?" As soon as Jesus heard the word that was spoken, He said to the ruler of the synagogue, 'Do not be afraid; only believe.'"* (Mark 5:35-36)

Jairus had a choice in that moment to believe the Lord or believe the messenger who had just been sent by the eyewitnesses who were with his daughter. Which word would carry more weight? Jesus immediately spoke to Jairus – "Do not be afraid; only believe." In essence, He was saying, "I know what you've seen Jairus, I know what you just heard from the messenger, but I need you to keep your eyes on Me. I need you to trust my word over every other word right now. Don't let that report bring any doubt into your mind, because I'm still headed to your house! I haven't changed My mind. I'm not swayed by this news, and I'm not too late. Just trust Me!"

"Preserve me, O God, for in You, I put my trust." (Psalm 16:1)

When we hear reports that seem impossible to overcome, we must not rely on our own understanding. The power of God defies all human reason. He is capable of doing more than we can ask, think or imagine!

"Trust in the Lord with all your heart, and lean not on your own understanding; in all your ways acknowledge Him, and He shall direct your paths" (Proverbs 3:5-6).

We must continue being grounded in this faith, standing steadfast in our hope in Christ, because He who has promised is faithful!

I AM WITH YOU!

One of the most deeply rooted beliefs (actually, "unbeliefs") is that God's presence is greater with some than with others. We make up all kinds of reasons to support this idea. We say that some are more holy, or more prayerful, or more prophetic. As if the presence of God depended upon us! The promise of His presence with us is unconditional! Let me say that again; His Presence with us is unconditional!

From the beginning God said,

"I will not leave you nor forsake you"

(Joshua 1:5).

He made this promise to Joshua, and the same promise was repeated 1,300 years later in Hebrews 13:5; *"I will never leave you, nor forsake you."*

To judge whether God is with people or not, we go by the wrong signs. We look at this person or that and judge by what he does or fails to do. God does not shrink or swell according to the person. Praise Jesus! He is no more with an evangelist than He is with a pastor. He is no more with a pastor than He is with a church member.

Moses had the most extraordinary experiences with God that a man ever had. Joshua could not share these experiences fully at the time. However, it was to Joshua that God said, "I will not leave you nor forsake you." The presence of God with us does not vary with our calling or with our successes. If God was only with us when we had success, success would never come!

In Matthew 28:20, Jesus said, *"And behold, I am with you always, to the end of the age."* When Jesus said, *"I am with you always,"* that wasn't only a promise – He was stating a fact! He was making a declaration about both the present day and all the days to come after it! He is with you right now, this very moment, and forevermore!

Rejoice!
You are never alone.
Jesus is with you!

DON'T PANIC

It takes more than survival skills to survive a crisis. For example, the ability to survive in a physical wilderness takes more than the skills to build a shelter, start a fire, and purify water. It requires a certain psychology, a mind-set, a will to live that overcomes the fear and stress associated with the crisis. In fact, some people who possessed the skill still died when stranded in a physical wilderness because they lacked the will to live. And others who lacked the skill but had the will, found a way to survive.

Upon entering a crisis, our tendency is often to let our imagination run wild. "Will I ever make it out?" "Why is this happening to me?" "I don't feel ready for this." "Does God not realize what I'm going through?" "Is He angry with me?" "Is He judging me?" "Is He even real?" Though it's natural to ask questions like these, obsessing over them depletes our resolve to believe God. And since these questions relate to the very nature of God, their responses must be biblically sound.

You see, perspective is everything. If you find yourself in a wilderness, if you find yourself in a crisis – physical, spiritual, or otherwise: don't panic. Take a deep breath. Take a moment to remind yourself who God is, who you are in Christ, and what the Bible says about His faithfulness during troubled times. Fear only makes you susceptible to lies from the enemy. He will lie about God's faithfulness and love for you. He'll even lie about God's existence, or about how valuable you are to Him. Such lies are meant to sap you of spiritual stamina. But that's just when the "will to live" must rise – the will to live in the Spirit while you pass through desert regions.

For God's children in the wilderness, the "will to live" does not merely refer to a desire to survive. It refers rather to an earnest determination to believe God. During spiritual drought, you must determine – sometimes against all circumstances, emotions, and even the advice of friends – that God is real. He is good! He is faithful, and you will make it through to the other side with Him. Don't let the enemy or circumstances define who God is for you. Refuse to allow yourself to believe anything but God's Word. Resolve as David did during a spiritual desert: *"My heart is steadfast, O God, my heart is steadfast!"* (Psalms 57:7).

One of the most important things you can understand is that even when it seems like everything around you is spinning out of control, if you are a child of God, there is nothing that touches your life that is not ultimately under God's supervision. Everything in your life is somehow "Father-filtered." He loves you dearly and deeply! He is watching over you, and won't allow anything to separate you from Him.

"For I am convinced that neither death nor life, neither angels nor demons, neither the present nor the future, nor any powers, neither height nor depth, nor anything else in all creation, will be able to separate us from the love of God that is in Christ Jesus our Lord" (Romans 8:38-39).

Allow God's invincible love to cast out all of your fear.

"Not only so, but we also glory in our sufferings, because we know that suffering produces perseverance; perseverance, character; and character, hope. And hope does not put us to shame, because God's love has been poured out into our hearts through the Holy Spirit, who has been given to us" (Romans 5:3-5).

WHO'S GOT YOUR BACK?

It is vitally important that every believer has a buddy in the body of Christ. The author of Hebrews said, *"Encourage one another day after day, as long as it is still called Today, so that none of you will be hardened by the deceitfulness of sin"* (Hebrews 3:13). When a person is isolated, they become especially vulnerable to discouragement and deception.

Have you ever watched a wildlife documentary where lions are hunting, on the Serengeti for instance? You will often see how a lion waits for one of the poor creatures on the fringes to separate itself from the herd. The lion will single out the one who strays away from the group because the lion knows that there is safety in numbers – and the devil knows this too. The Bible says that the devil prowls around like a roaring lion looking for someone to devour. Those who isolate themselves become an easy meal for Satan. In times of pain and hardship, without the support of the body, he knows that we can easily fall prey to his temptations and traps.

One day as I was reading about the "armor of God" in Ephesians 6,I had a revelation. The passage tells us that God has provided armor for the head, the feet, the chest, and the waist; and He has also given us a shield and a sword. But then I saw something I had never noticed before – all the protection is facing forward – there is no armor protecting the back! At first, I found this very peculiar and then suddenly verse 18 jumped out at me, *"Praying always with all prayer and supplication in the Spirit and watching thereunto with all perseverance for all saints."* This verse, which is mentioned in the context of the armor of God, says that we are supposed to be looking out for one another and defending each other in the battle. There is no back armor because we are supposed to have each other's backs. If God equipped us in such a way that we need others to watch our backs, then it is clear that He never intended that we go into battle alone.

God created us to need one another.

This is why if you are going through a trial, a battle, a crisis, or a barren season, you need to surround yourself with brothers and sisters who will pray for you and watch out for you with purpose and perseverance. We all need each other, especially in these last days leading up to the return of Jesus! I want to encourage you to find ways to stay connected to the people God has placed in your life.

THE COMFORTER

Who is a more faithful comrade in hardships than the Holy Spirit? Whose friendship is more valuable during troubled times than the most wonderful, kind, loyal, and awesome confidante in the universe? When taking stock of your resources, remember this most precious, personal gift of His presence and fellowship. The living God, in the Person of the Holy Spirit, is going before you, walking beside you, guarding behind you, resting upon you, and dwelling within you! What more do you need?

The greater our revelation of the Holy Spirit's presence, the greater our comfort. And the greater our comfort, the less the suffering feels like suffering. This is not to say that the Holy Spirit will inoculate us from all pain and distress. Instead, it means the depth of the Holy Spirit's comfort enables us, not only to maintain our joy and character in the trying times, but also to flourish there in Christ more than ever.

"The wilderness and the dry land shall be glad; the desert shall rejoice and blossom like the crocus; it shall blossom abundantly and rejoice with joy and singing... Then the eyes of the blind shall be opened, and the ears of the deaf unstopped; then shall the lame man leap like a deer, and the tongue of the mute sing for joy. For waters break forth in the wilderness, and streams in the desert; the burning sand shall become a pool, and the thirsty ground springs of water; in the haunt of jackals, where they lie down, the grass shall become reeds and rushes"(Isaiah 35:1-2, 5-7).

How can we have a "wilderness" so colorful, alive, and exhilarating? Through the comforting, transforming presence of the Holy Spirit! This is what makes the wilderness totally worth the trouble. It gives us the opportunity to experience the Holy Spirit's comfort on a level we would never have experienced otherwise.

Nothing is more valuable than the awareness of the ever-present God.

If you feel as though you have entered a wilderness, determine you will use this as an occasion to discover more about the magnificent reality of the Holy Spirit.

THE LONG ARM OF THE LORD

My friend, no matter how daunting your problem or need may seem right now, be assured that in reality, it is a small matter of very little true significance. Why should the omnipotent, omnipresent, omniscient, eternal God intervene in our affairs of such utter triviality? Because God uses our lives as a platform from which He desires to receive praise and glory.

From the day we are born until the day we die, our lives exist for one reason – to glorify God.

Take, for example, Peter's imprisonment in Acts chapter 12. It was a crisis that could have ended in catastrophe or victory. To the believers gathered in Mary's house praying for his release, their primary concerns were most likely immediate. They were frightened that they would lose the great apostle who was also their friend and leader. They were probably empathetic with Peter's suffering and the brutal execution he was facing. But there was a more enduring matter at stake – the eternal glory of God. The intercessors probably had no idea that through their prayers God would unleash His power in an extraordinary way that would be a testimony to many generations – including ours. How many thousands have been inspired by this amazing story of Peter's supernatural escape from prison? Yet, it might have been a tragic tale lost to history had it not been for the prayers of those few fervent prayer warriors standing in the gap.

God is primarily concerned with receiving glory from our lives. Perhaps the daunting circumstances you are facing are just a platform from which God desires to demonstrate a mighty miracle to an unbelieving world!

"For the eyes of the LORD range throughout the earth to strengthen those whose hearts are fully committed to him." (2 Chronicle 16:9a)

He wants to receive glory through your sickness. He wants to receive praise through your financial emergency. He wants to receive honor through your family situation. Call upon the Lord! Inquire of Him. Ask Him what He thinks and desires. Don't lean on the arm of the flesh. Don't deprive Him of the opportunity to be your „*very present help in trouble.*" Come to Him with the situation you are facing today, and He will display His glory in and through your life!

Friend, it's time to pray. There is nothing too difficult for the omnipresent Holy Spirit. Isaiah 59:1 says, *„The Lord's arm is not so short that he cannot save"*.

Although Peter was imprisoned on the other side of town, through prayer in the name of Jesus, the physical chains on his hands were loosed and all barriers were removed. When you pray, you have the power to bring deliverance to the oppressed. You can have a real impact that reaches to the ends of the earth without ever even leaving home. What you bind on earth will be bound in heaven – what you loose on earth will be loosed in heaven. No door, no chain, no barrier, and no distance are too great for the long arm of the Lord!

YOUR FATHER WILL NOT LET YOU DROWN

Pleasure over pain is our default setting, and we are usually looking for the path of least resistance. But unlike us God sees our lives from the vantage point of eternity, and His primary concern is not our comfort but our conforming to the image of His Son. How effective do you think an army would be if the soldiers were trained at five-star resorts? How reliable would a scholar be if he never took a test? How long would a boxer last in the ring if his training consisted of pillow fights?

I read about a scientific experiment that involved a group of researchers who had isolated themselves from the outside world in an artificial environment called a "biosphere." Inside the biosphere the scientists had successfully replicated nearly every weather condition on earth except for one – wind. To their surprise, the absence of wind was disastrous for the trees, which began to bend and snap under their own weight. It turns out that wind strengthens the trees by creating stress! Without this resistance the trees will not develop enough strength to hold themselves upright. This is the common law of life.

Several years ago, when our kids were still toddlers, my wife and I lived in a house with a swimming pool that we enjoyed very much. But I was always concerned that one of the children might fall into the pool when an adult was not looking. So out of concern for their safety I enrolled my son and daughter in swimming lessons. The first few days were a torment, for them and for us, because learning to swim is a baptism by fire. I am sure my kids thought their teacher was trying to drown them. They cried, they resisted, they protested, and they pleaded for deliverance. But when they looked at us, their parents, we were sitting on the sidelines silently. We watched their struggle, and our hearts were aching to see their distress, but we would not intervene. This challenge was for their own good, and we allowed it because of our love for them. But all the time they were struggling and suffering, our loving eyes were trained on them. We watched their every movement and would never have allowed them to drown.

Just before Moses died he sang a song over Israel and said, "*He* [the Lord] *found him* [Israel] *in a desert land, in the howling void of the wilderness; He kept circling around him, He scanned him* [penetratingly], *He kept him as the pupil of His eye*" (Deuteronomy 32:10).

Moses, Israel, David, and countless others – including Jesus Himself – passed through the wilderness as they followed the call of God. The difficulties they encountered and the trials they faced were all a part of God's plan and were used to accomplish God's purpose for their lives. Being in God's will does not mean there will never be setbacks or that we will be immune to difficulty.

But even in the midst of the wilderness, God will spread His wings over us and keep circling around us as an eagle flutters over her young.

God loves us!

He will keep us as the apple of His eye, and He will never allow us to drown.

A PRAYER OF AGREEMENT

Does prayer really make a difference? Can we really alter the outcome of situations and circumstances through prayer? Someone once said that prayer doesn't change things, it only changes the person praying, but this is completely contrary to Scripture. Prayer does change situations because God has made us partners with Him for the fulfillment of His purposes in the earth and prayer is one fundamental way in which we partner with God. The prophet Elijah is a great example of this principle.

For three years and six months Israel had been plagued by famine until God promised the prophet that He would send rain. *"And it came to pass after many days, that the word of the Lord came to Elijah in the third year saying, ,Go show thyself to Ahab and I will send rain upon the earth'"* (1 Kings 18:1). But at the end of the same chapter in which the promise was given, we see Elijah praying for the fulfillment of the promise. He cast himself down on the ground and put his face between his knees. Seven times he sent his servant to look for any sign of rain and in the meantime James 5:17 tells us that he ‚'prayed earnestly". One might wonder why Elijah needed to pray at all if God had already promised that He would send the answer. But Elijah understood that the promise required partnership through prayer.

Oh, how many promises there are to the child of God who will only take a hold of them earnestly through faith and prayer. Yes! Prayer does matter. It has the power to change the world. There is a great need for prayer in the world right now! The Bible shows us that our Heavenly Father moves in power on our behalf when we pray together in agreement! *"Again I say to you that if two of you agree on earth concerning anything that they ask, it will be done for them by My Father in heaven"* (Matthew 18:19). Faith is not even mentioned in this verse. In fact, the only requirement for the Lord to do what we ask, is for there to be more than one in agreement! Will you be my plus one, and join me in a prayer of agreement over the earth right now? Let's pray this aloud together:

Father in heaven, we come before you from all around the globe, to agree with one another that your will would be done on earth as it is in heaven. We humble ourselves on behalf of the nations and ask you to please forgive us of our sins and cleanse us from all unrighteousness. We ask for a great harvest of souls to be saved in this hour and that Your glory would cover the earth as the water covers the sea! Holy Spirit come and comfort all those who are suffering and heal every sickness and disease. Lord Jesus we ask you to rebuke the enemy on our behalf and drive back the powers of darkness with your mighty right hand. Thank you for being our peace that passes all understanding in every circumstance we face – you guard our hearts and our minds. Thank you for the cross! You have already won the war over the enemy! We come together in agreement for all these things and lay hold of the victory that You have already laid hold of for us! Thank you and praise you for all you have done and all you are doing now! In Jesus' Name, Amen.

THE SHELTER OF HIS PRESENCE

Even in dire circumstances, amid turmoil and chaos, you can remain hidden in Christ, shielded and safe within an impenetrable fortress made of walls a thousand miles thick. He is a still, enclosed garden amid the chaos outside. He will keep your spirit stable as if you were not really under such extreme conditions.

"They will neither hunger nor thirst, nor will the desert heat or the sun beat down on them" (Isaiah 49:10).

How can this be? How can our most vulnerable time be our most protected and durable time? Because God *"is our refuge and strength, a very present help in trouble"* (Psalms 46:1).

"Whoever dwells in the shelter of the Most High will rest in the shadow of the Almighty. I will say of the Lord, 'He is my refuge and my fortress, my God, in whom I trust.' Surely he will save you from the fowler's snare and from the deadly pestilence. He will cover you with his feathers, and under his wings you will find refuge; his faithfulness will be your shield and rampart. You will not fear the terror of night, nor the arrow that flies by day, nor the pestilence that stalks in the darkness, nor the plague that destroys at midday. A thousand may fall at your side, ten thousand at your right hand, but it will not come near you. You will only observe with your eyes and see the punishment of the wicked. If you say, 'The Lord is my refuge,' and you make the Most High your dwelling, no harm will overtake you, no disaster will come near your tent" (Psalms 91:1-10).

Think about this. When did God first promise He would abide with His people? When did He establish His presence with them? When did He give specific instructions for building His tabernacle in the middle of their camp? In the wilderness! That was the very time He inaugurated His personal, permanent presence with Israel. To this day Jews celebrate the "Feast of Booths," a festival celebrating the season when they lived in tents in the wilderness, and God lived in a tent among them. The wilderness is not the place of God's absence. It is the place where He establishes His presence in a fresh way. The place of His presence is with you! Right where you are at – He is your refuge and fortress!

People often say that God's presence is more real to their souls in the midst of troubling times than usual. In the middle of great pain and suffering, they come to know the presence of Jesus in a deeper more powerful and personal way than they had ever experienced before. No matter how discouraged you may be feeling – rouse yourself to seek the Lord. Make His faithfulness your shield and shelter. Wrap yourself in His truth and love.

Spend time in His presence and in His Word and know that you are hidden in a powerful fortress that the darkness cannot penetrate.

"Even though I walk through the valley of the shadow of death, I will fear no evil, for you are with me; your rod and your staff, they comfort me. You prepare a table before me in the presence of my enemies; you anoint my head with oil; my cup overflows. Surely goodness and mercy shall follow me all the days of my life, and I shall dwell in the house of the Lord forever." (Psalm 23:4-6)

FACE YOUR FEAR

After Moses died, his protégé, Joshua, became the new leader. God promised to be with Joshua as He had been with Moses. God promised to give Joshua every place upon which the sole of his foot would tread. God promised to prosper Joshua wherever he went. But there was one requirement: *"Only be strong and very courageous,"* the Lord said (Joshua 1:7).

Imagine you are about to embark on the most challenging undertaking of your life. You have no idea what lies before you, and then the Lord comes to you and says,

"Be very courageous."

That would scare me! Why? Because courage is only needed in the presence of danger. Courage is not the absence of fear. In fact, there is no courage without fear. Courage is the willingness to face fear with faith. All the promises, victories, and destiny awaiting Joshua were dependent on his willingness to face his fear.

When I was a teenager, I went to England on a missions trip, and stayed in a "host home" with a lovely British couple. They had a poster hanging on their wall that is forever branded in my mind's eye. The poster showed a group of ten-year-olds, twenty-year-olds, thirty-year-olds, all the way up to hundred-year-olds, and each was asked the same question: "What is your number one regret at this point in your life?" All the answers were both interesting and funny – but the only answer that struck my heart and forever burned itself into my memory, was the answer of those who were a hundred years old. Their number one regret at that point in their life, was that they "should have taken more risks." I determined then, as a very young man, that when I come to the end of my life, I don't want to look back and realize that I never really lived at all because I was always too afraid.

Fear always seems legitimate in the moment, but when one looks back over the course of their life at the things they used to worry about – it becomes evident quite quickly that they should have taken more risks for the Lord's sake. Fear is never a good excuse to not do God's will. The parable of the talents in Matthew chapter 25 illustrates this.

A wealthy man was planning to go away on a long journey. Before he left, he decided to divide his money among his three servants so they could invest it and his fortune would increase while he was away. The first two servants invested their money wisely, and the master was pleased when he returned. But the third servant said, *"I was afraid, and went out and hid your talent in the ground"* (Matthew 25:25). He buried his talent because of fear. The master didn't respond with, "There, there, it's alright, you poor little servant. I'm so sorry I put you in an uncomfortable position." No, the master rebuked him sharply with anger and said, "You wicked and lazy servant!" The master was angry with him because rather than facing his fears and taking a risk for the master's sake, he chose to take the easy path: bury the talent and do nothing.

The time is ticking away on the clock, and soon our master will return. What is at stake is God's eternal kingdom. He has entrusted the advancement of His kingdom into our hands, and one day He will return and we will give an account for what we've done with His investment. If we have any reason to fear - it is only this, that our lives would produce Him nothing more than a buried bag of talents. Our lives do not belong to us – they belong to our Master, our Lord and Savior, who risked everything for our sake. May we risk everything for His sake in return, that He would receive the reward of His suffering.

I love the way Jim Elliot put it:

"He is no fool who gives what he cannot keep to gain what he cannot lose."

Jesus said, *"For whoever wants to save their life will lose it, but whoever loses their life for me will find it."* You cannot fail when giving Jesus your all! Fear is only an illusion! You risk nothing when you risk your life for the Master. Instead, you will only hear, *"Well done, my good and faithful servant! You have been faithful with a few things; I will put you in charge of many things. Come and share your master's happiness!"* (Matthew 25:23).

EXPECT A MIRACLE!

The angel suddenly vanished and a cool morning breeze sent a chill down Peter's arm. Suddenly he realized that he was awake and everything he had just experienced was real. He had been in a Roman prison where an angel was sent to deliver him (Acts 12). The chains had really fallen from his wrists. He had really walked right past the guards. The huge iron gates had really opened and he was really free!

Knowing that the believers were praying for him, he made his way through the empty streets to the house of Mary, the mother of John Mark. This is where the prayer meeting was being held, and Peter could hardly wait to show his face to his dear friends who were diligently interceding for his release. This is where the story becomes a bit comical because while all the other barriers and doors had opened to Peter so freely, he was about to encounter one door that would not open to him. The Bible says in Acts 12:13 that Peter knocked at the gate and a young lady named Rhoda heard it. She came to the door, and through the crack she asked, "Who's there?" Peter said, "It's me, Rhoda... I've just been delivered from prison. Open the door and let me come in." Rhoda was so excited to hear Peter's voice that she failed to open the door. She ran back into the room where the prayer meeting was in full swing. Some were bowing, others were weeping, still others were warring in the heavenlies for Peter's release. Rhoda interrupted the prayer meeting with the urgent announcement, "Hey, everybody! Peter is at the door!" They laughed at her. "You're crazy, Rhoda... don't you know that Peter is in prison? He is bound between two soldiers, behind two wards of guards, behind a massive iron gate. Peter couldn't possibly be at the door. Now get back in here and pray!" She kept insisting it was Peter, but they said, "It is his angel!"

I'm not sure how long the debate continued, but the Bible does tell us that all the while this discussion was taking place, Peter continued knocking. What a comical irony! Every door had opened to Peter except the door of the house where the believers were praying for the doors to open. This illustrates a powerful point. God has given us the keys to the kingdom. He has made us the doorkeeper. What we bind in heaven will be bound on earth... what we loose in heaven will be loosed on earth. We have the power and authority to open every door.

There is no power on earth that can stand against us, and the very gates of hell itself will not prevail.

But there is one door that can always stand in our way and keep us from receiving our miracle. It is the door of unbelief.

So often the answer to our prayers has been standing on our own front porch, but we have missed it because we did not believe that God had actually heard and answered us. The believers were praying for Peter, but apparently, they did not believe that God would answer them. The only thing worse than prayerlessness is prayer without expectation.

DRINK DEEPLY AND OFTEN

Survival experts tell us not to wait until we feel thirsty before we drink water – because by then, our bodies are already dehydrated. We are told to drink as much as possible to keep the hydration level of our bodies high. In severe cases of dehydration, doctors will prescribe an IV (intravenous rehydration) for those who have become dangerously dehydrated.

Just as water is a critical source for our natural bodies, our spirits are dependent upon God's spirit. "You, God, are my God, earnestly I seek you. I thirst for you, my whole being longs for you, in a dry and parched land where there is no water" (Psalms 63:1). Just as the Holy Spirit is our comforter, He is also our refreshment and the life sustainer for our innermost being. Jesus said, "If anyone is thirsty, let him come to Me and drink. He who believes in Me, as the scripture said, *"From his innermost being will flow rivers of living water"* (John 7:37-38).

Jude tells us as believers facing trouble, *"You, beloved,"* keep yourselves in God's love by, *"building yourselves up on your most holy faith, praying in the Holy Spirit"* (Jude 20-21). Just as water rehydrates our physical bodies, praying in tongues edifies our spirit man. The verb, "edify," means more than just "encourage." The original word actually means "to construct, strengthen, or restore." In other words, through speaking in tongues, the Spirit not only encourages our hearts, but also builds up our inner person. Just like an IV delivers fluid directly into a vein, bypassing the digestive system, praying in tongues enables us to bypass our minds and pray straight from our spirit! Praying in the Spirit is a direct connection to God's hydrating power! *"For one who speaks in a tongue, speaks not to men but to God..."* (1 Corinthians 14:2a).

The Holy Spirit has a broad treasury of language for every kind of situation and emotion we may face. He's got the answer to every problem known to mankind! When we pray in the Spirit, we move ourselves in closer proximity to the Lord to hear His voice and cooperate with His specific expression in any given moment. When God answers these prayers from our spirit, we receive measures of peace, joy, and strength that can come no other way. These are the virtues that fortify us from within, filling us with living water from the internal springs of His Spirit. We become spiritually healthy people, full of faith and spiritual vitality for others.

Drink deeply and often of your internal resources by praying in the Spirit.

DIVINE POWER IN ACTION

Did you know that when people talk of Christianity as a world religion, they are quite wrong? A religion is a system, and Jesus left no system. It is more than just a faith to be believed. The real thing is actually divine power in action. *"But you will receive power when the Holy Spirit has come upon you"* (Acts 1:5-8).

Christian truth cannot simply be written down like so many facts or definitions. Christian truth is alive. You cannot write a person down and say, "That's her!" You cannot write Christianity down and say, "That's it!" It is a living entity. The breath of God animates the Gospel, or it is a dead body of truth instead of living truth. Jesus said, *"I am the way, the truth, and the life"* (John 14:6). That is how I know it, and that is how I preach it. Who would not want to preach a Gospel like that?

Christianity is the Holy Spirit in action making the Word of God happen. The baptism in the Spirit was not meant to be a single, emotional event recorded in believers' diaries. It wraps around believers permanently. The Spirit is their environment, the air that they breathe moment by moment, providing the vitality of the Christian faith. When we bombard the world with the Gospel, the Holy Spirit is the explosive ammunition for our artillery. The Spirit animates believers, their teachings, their preaching, their prayer, their service, and their very lives.

The Holy Spirit is the dynamic of the faith.

Without the life of the Holy Spirit, Christianity is just another lifeless religious system that can only be kept going by human effort. But nothing can compete with the Holy Spirit. We cannot do without the Holy Spirit no matter what we substitute, whether organization, church magnificence, prestige, education, or any other factor on which reliance has been placed.

We must be able to show people that the Gospel is what it claims to be.

When a world-class athlete stands on the track, we do not need to argue to prove that he is a champion. Just fire the starting pistol! That is what I do – the Gospel of Christ is alive, so I go into a stadium and let the Gospel do its own thing, and everybody can see it is alive. That is what the Holy Spirit does.

At this point I think I should illustrate what I have declared by actual examples. Once, during a service in Brazzaville, the capital of the Republic of Congo, God gave me a word of knowledge for a couple, otherwise unknown to me, somewhere among the tens of thousands present. There was a woman who had been in a coma for three days and had been carried into the meeting by her husband. By faith and in obedience to God's prompting, I told the vast audience what the Spirit of the Lord had made known to me. As I spoke, the unconscious woman, though not hearing, came out of her coma and was healed. Mind over matter? Impossible – the patient knew nothing of what was going on until she revived.

Another poor soul also present needed urgent surgery. Her unborn baby had died in her womb, and the hospital had arranged for it to be removed the next day. When a prayer was offered for the mass of needy ones in the service, the baby in her womb leaped. She rushed forward to the platform tearfully to testify, and only just in time, because straight afterward she went into labor and was taken away to give birth to a bouncing baby boy!

These are just a couple of the wonders out of many, that have left me almost unable to sleep for excitement and joy. Infinitely greater is that the Holy Spirit sweeps through the vast crowds assembled to hear the Word of God like a mighty heavenly dam-burst and lifts them on a wave of blessing into the kingdom of God.

THE FAITHFUL ONE

Fear cannot exist in the same time and space as faith. Many believers have a past tense faith; they believe God has done things. In fact, most people can believe anything if it took place a long time ago or will take place far in the future. They can accept a promise like,

"All things work together for good to those who love God" (Romans 8:28),

which might mean eternity. But they find it harder to believe, *"I am the Lord who heals you"* (Exodus 15:26). They have a past faith but not a present faith. This leaves a dangerous gap for doubt, fear, and unbelief, in the present tense.

Many believe in the faithful God of Moses and Elijah; they believe Jesus worked miracles and the Holy Spirit empowered the disciples. But that is empty faith unless it transfers to today, unless they believe He will carry on the good work in their present life.

One man with the message of a past, present, and future faith was John the apostle. When he was up against the whole Roman Empire, he wrote a marvelous and triumphant book. He said, *"I, John, both your brother and companion in the tribulation and kingdom and patience of Jesus Christ, was on the island that is called Patmos for the word of God and for the testimony of Jesus Christ"* (Revelation 1:9). John was close to Jesus in a unique way. He also suffered for Christ. And John was the man who saw what things meant; He read the signs with prophetic insight. What he saw was difficult to explain. It was new on earth. Nobody had thought of what he said in Revelation 1:4-5: *"Grace to you and peace from Him who is and who was and who is to come, and from the seven Spirits who are before His throne, and from Jesus Christ, the faithful witness, the firstborn from the dead, and the ruler over the kings of the earth."* How can Jesus be a faithful witness? We are witnesses to Christ, but to what does Christ witness? This Scripture refers back to another passage: *"The Pharisees therefore said to Him, "You bear witness of Yourself; Your witness is not true." Jesus answered and said to them, "Even if I bear witness of Myself, My witness is true, for I know where I came from and where I am going; but you do not know where I come from and where I am going... I am One who bears witness of Myself, and the Father who sent Me bears witness of Me"* (John 8:13-14, 18).

Jesus witnesses to Himself. He said, *"You believe in God, believe also in Me"* (John 14:1). By His life and mighty deeds, He has shown us who He is. He witnesses to who He is. He is faithful to what He said about Himself, and He does not disappoint us. If He was different now, in the present tense, He would not be a faithful witness. But His actions are consistent with what He said. Jesus' life spells hope for the sick, the lonely, the lost, and the hopeless. We must have faith in Him for the present moment, not just in "who was" and "who is to come."

He is the God "who is" right now!

His faithfulness has never ceased, or even paused. He is the Faithful One now and forevermore!

LIFE IN THE SPIRIT

The Bible says, *"For God has not given us a spirit of fear, but of power and of love and of a sound mind."* (2 Timothy 1:7)

As born-again believers, we don't live our lives according to the flesh, but according to the Spirit.

"There is therefore now no condemnation to those who are in Christ Jesus, who do not walk according to the flesh, but according to the Spirit." (Romans 8:1)

The entire Christian life is "in the Spirit." By the Spirit, the Son of God is the Anointed One. This set the pattern. Just as He went about doing good because He was anointed with the Spirit, so must we all. We are told to walk (as Jesus did everywhere) in the Spirit, pray in the Spirit, love in the Spirit, live in the Spirit, be filled with the Spirit, sing in the Spirit, and have the fruit of the Spirit. The Spirit-filled life is not an experience to be cultivated only in special conditions like indoor flowers. Christians are not flowers.

During the early expansion of the industrial cities of England some clergymen could not be persuaded to take a parish among the hordes of unwashed workers, because they said it might spoil their "spirituality." The Holy Spirit makes believers tough specimens for all conditions. They carry perpetual springtime in their soul and are "winterized" (as Americans describe the preparation of their homes for the cold weather).

When the Holy Spirit came, the apostles discovered a new resilience, a new strength within them, and a power that operated in their weakness, which sent them out into a brutalized, pagan world to demolish its idol establishment and change history. That is a true mark of "the Spirit-filled life." Things like that are happening today.

The baptism in the Spirit makes God's people unconquerable!

BELIEVING GOD'S PROMISES

God pledged to Israel that He would give them a land flowing with milk and honey. He promised them a good and spacious land where they would enjoy security and have rest from their enemies. Indeed, He would liberate them from bondage and personally escort them into the home of their dreams Himself. This was His promise, His "word" to them.

After centuries of slavery in Egypt, what exhilaration they must have felt when they "heard" this promise. What delight they must have taken in the dream-come true "word" declaring their own country, identity, and freedom. Yet here they were in a desert – no milk, no honey, no safety, no inheritance, no promise fulfilled. Months earlier, as the Red Sea parted before their eyes, God's promises must have felt so real to them! They must have almost tasted their Land's fruit and smelled its lilies. But instead: dust, danger, rocks, thirst, serpents, and fears – the desert. God said, "Promised Land," but then He led them into the wilderness. Instead of entering their glory, they were wandering in a wasteland, battling cruel elements, and scrounging for strange food every morning.

Israel faced a predicament. The word of God that promised a glorious future now looked absurd in the barren wilderness of shattered dreams. The "word they heard," instead of inspiring hope through fulfillment, now seemed to hang suspended above them, just out of reach, sneering and jeering at them as they roamed the desert. So, Israel no longer believed "the word they heard." They rejected God's promise that they would enter the Land of their destiny!

Israel was caught in that long, strange tension between promise and fulfillment, between God's integrity and circumstances that appeared to contradict His Word. But that was the very time they needed to believe! If they would have believed God's Word amid such crisis, then they would have obeyed it and profited from it. Since they did not believe, they did not obey – and did not receive its benefits. God put them in this situation and watched to see what kind of people He had. When we are faced with circumstances that seem to contradict the promises God has given us in His word, we must choose to believe above all else, He is faithful to His word and to us!

We must not allow fear, doubt, or unbelief to set in, because when God makes a promise, it *will* come to pass!

GOD SEES MORE IN YOU THAN YOU SEE IN YOURSELF

The Bible describes the Midianites as a nation of "grasshoppers" (Judges 7:12). Whenever the harvest was ripe, they would descend upon Israel's fields and crops in vast numbers like a swarm of locusts, leaving nothing in their wake but destruction and desolation. The Israelites went on the defensive, hunkering down in caves, hiding in the mountains, and building protective strongholds. The nervous harvesters quickly reaped what they could and hid it away in anticipation of an imminent invasion.

God had a plan to deliver Israel from the hand of Midian, and He had chosen just the man for the job, but God's choice seemed highly unlikely. Gideon was not a superhero by any stretch of the imagination. He was a victim of his society's ills, a man who had been influenced by the climate of cowardice that had crippled and enslaved the Israelites. He was such a prisoner of fear that he would hide in a winepress to thresh his small harvest of wheat (Judges 6:11).

A winepress is no place to thresh wheat; it's like washing your clothes in the dishwasher. But Gideon had chosen this inappropriate place because he was afraid of the Midianites. He was afraid of losing his harvest and his life, so he hid both underground. It was in this dungeon of fear that the Lord found Gideon, frustrated, trembling, and perspiring.

"And the Angel of the Lord appeared to him and said to him, The Lord is with you, you mighty man of [fearless] *courage."* (Judges 6:12)

No one would have anticipated the Lord's declaration that day. "Gideon," the Lord says, "you are a mighty man of fearless courage!" Where others saw a coward, God saw a deliverer! I'm so glad God doesn't see us the way we so often see ourselves. When we look in the mirror, we might see someone who is undereducated or inexperienced. We might see someone who belongs to the wrong social class, race, or gender. We might see someone who is too young or too old. And there are always a million excuses why God can't use us. But God sees more in us than we see in ourselves, and our obstacles, failures, and shortcomings do not intimidate Him. Why? Because though we are weak, He is strong!

2 Corinthians 12:9 says, "And He has said to me,

"My grace is sufficient for you, for power is perfected in weakness."

Most gladly, therefore, I will rather boast about my weaknesses, so that the power of Christ may dwell in me."

In the winepress we find a trembling, perspiring coward hiding for his life when the Angel of the Lord appears to Gideon and calls him a "mighty man of [fearless] courage." At first those words almost sound like cruel sarcasm, but there was no smirk on the angel's face. God was not mocking Gideon, nor did He have Gideon confused with someone else. God saw something in Gideon that no one else saw, including Gideon himself. How comforting it is to know that God's ways are not our ways and His thoughts are not our thoughts. Oh, my friend, when you understand what God sees when He looks at you, it will change your life.

THE STRUGGLE IS REAL

One day a little boy happened upon a butterfly trying to break out of its cocoon. The little boy decided to help the struggling butterfly, but after tearing the cocoon open, he discovered that the butterfly inside was shriveled and weak – so frail, in fact, that it soon died. What the little boy did not realize, is that pushing against the cocoon was a necessary part of the butterfly's development. Without the struggle the cocoon provided, the butterfly would not have the strength to survive when it emerged.

God doesn't ever do anything to harm us, but He uses the difficulties that come into our lives, to teach us faith, to refine our character, and to equip us for the greater challenges that lie ahead. *"If you have raced with men on foot and they have tired you out, then how can you compete with horses?"* (Jeremiah 12:5).

Right now, across the globe, many people are facing some pretty difficult circumstances, for all kinds of reasons. Some have lost jobs, some face persecution, some have lost loved ones, and some are fighting for their very lives. For those who belong to Christ, no season of life – no matter how difficult, is wasted.

God will cause everything to work together for your good, because you love Him and because you are called according to His purpose (Romans 8:28).

My friend, something important is happening in your life right now. Your faith is being stretched, and your patience is being tried. Your spiritual ears are being tuned as you listen to hear the voice of God's Spirit. You are confronting doubts and questions. You may be going through a great struggle, but that struggle is all part of the process of birthing all God wants to do in your life. God always prepares us in advance for what He has in store for us! That process may be uncomfortable, but it is necessary nonetheless.

Get ready. Good things are coming for you!

FEAR PARALYZES, BUT FAITH LEADS TO ACTION!

People can easily become paralyzed by fear. If a person is feeling extremely anxious or afraid about something in particular, they will go out of their way to avoid whatever triggers more of that same feeling. If you're dominated by anxieties, you will put off handling anything you believe might cause more anxiety. For example, some people are so afraid of failure, they will not take even one step towards success because they deem it as being too risky. But the real failure would be not realizing that if they never try, they forever miss the chance to succeed.

One day I went with my father to the shooting range. He was heading out on a hunting trip, and before he left, I wanted to help him "sight in" the rifle I had bought him as a gift. We looked through the scope, which we had just attached, aimed at the target, and fired, knowing that we would most likely miss the bullseye. But by firing at the target, we could see where we needed to make an adjustment to the scope. We were only able to make corrections when we saw how we were missing the mark. I think this is typical of life. We usually learn more from our mistakes than our successes. But unless you fire, you will never miss, and unless you miss, you will never be able to make the adjustments necessary to hit the bullseye.

Whenever I begin a new project or initiative, I never view my initial plan as the final draft. I dive into it knowing that I will learn as I go. This means that I'm not paralyzed by a fear of failure; rather I am looking forward to learning what not to do. I see my initial plan as an uncalibrated machine with many dials. The dials are all the different variables represented in that particular project. Once the machine is running, I can see what is working and what is not working. I am diligent to gather sufficient feedback, and then I will begin to tweak the "dials" based on that feedback. Even when I feel like everything is running smoothly, I will continue to step back often to analyze the process. If something is working well, I will try to capitalize on it. If something is not working well, I will adjust it or prune it off altogether. It is an ongoing dynamic development that never ends. You see, the process is where real progress is made, but until you take action, all of your planning and strategizing is simply untested theory.

Having said all these things, let me be clear: taking action is not just a matter of trial and error. At its core, it is a matter of faithfulness.

Success comes when practical strategies are coupled together with faith and good character.

Even if there are a thousand things you cannot do for one reason or another, there is always something you can do. It may seem small or insignificant, but the eyes of God are on you. He is watching to see what you will do with the opportunities He has given you, and your response will determine whether He entrusts you with more.

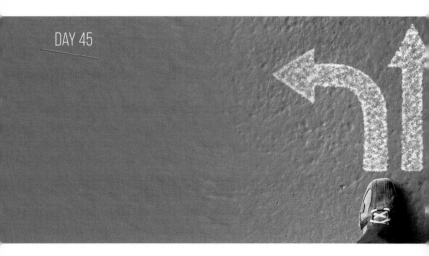

CAST THE DOUBT OUT!

I think many of God's people don't realize how sinister and dangerous unbelief is. Many pious and self-righteous Christians look down their religious noses at people committing other, more visible sins. They criticize them sharply without realizing that the unbelief they harbor in their hearts, and in some cases enshrine in their doctrines, is more wicked in God's sight than the sins they are condemning. Jesus rebuked His disciples for unbelief more than any other thing. The reason unbelief is so dangerous is that not only is it a sin in itself, but it also can be a gateway for other sins as well. We know faith is the currency of God's kingdom, and without faith it is impossible to please God (Hebrews 11:6).

However, I think many people have a basic misunderstanding about faith. They pray and seek more and more faith. But what if I told you that you already have plenty of faith? The problem is not that you have too little faith; the problem is that you have too much unbelief!

In Mark 9:24, a man said to Jesus, *"I do believe; help me overcome my unbelief!"* Notice that he didn't ask Jesus to give him more faith. In fact, he said, "I do believe." This man recognized that the problem was not too little faith but too much unbelief! Faith and unbelief can be present at the same time. Faith has the potential to move mountains, but unbelief will nullify the power of faith.

Let me explain it like this. When my wife was in Bible college, she owned a silver diesel Volkswagen Jetta. One day she lent the car to a friend. On his way to return the car, as a courtesy he decided to refill the fuel he had used. He pulled into the gas station, inserted his credit card, opened the cap of the gas tank, and began to fill it—with gasoline! How he missed the bold red warning on the tank that said to use "DIESEL FUEL ONLY" I will never know. But one thing is certain; his little mistake was costly for us and devastating for the vehicle.

After the gasoline was added, the vehicle would no longer run. It's not that there was too little diesel in the tank. The problem was the injection of a substance that was incompatible with the vehicle's design. This is exactly how unbelief works! The devil wants to inject unbelief into our spirits because he knows it will bring us to a screeching halt.

Let us consider the context of the verse where Jesus talked about mountain-moving faith. The story is found in Matthew 17:14-21. A certain man with a demon-possessed son had come to Jesus's disciples for help, but when they could not cast out the evil spirits, they asked Jesus why they had been so unsuccessful. He said to them, "Because of your unbelief". This is a very clear and precise explanation that Jesus reiterated by going on to say,

"If you have faith the size of a mustard seed, you will say to this mountain, 'Move from here to there,' and it will move; and nothing will be impossible to you."

So far this seems very straightforward. But the simplicity and clarity of this statement is often overshadowed by confusion over the next words Jesus spoke: *"However, this kind does not go out except by prayer and fasting."* (verse 21). It almost sounds as if Jesus contradicted Himself. When asked why the disciples had not been able to exorcize the demon, He said it was because of unbelief. But now He seems to be saying that it is because they had not fasted and prayed enough. Which is it? The confusion comes when we fail to realize the moral of the story.

At first glance it may appear that the demon is the focal point of this account, but a closer look will reveal that the real antagonist in this story is not the demon but the spirit of unbelief! The disciples were concerned about the demon inside the boy, but Jesus was concerned about the unbelief inside His disciples. The disciples' question was about casting out demons, but Jesus' answer was about casting out doubt. Jesus knew that once unbelief has been cast out, exorcizing demons would be a piece of cake!

Sometimes we have to pray long prayers and fast for many days before we get the victory, but it is not because our appeals coerce God into doing something. And it is not because we have finally earned the answer to our prayers by logging enough credit hours into our spiritual bank account. Much fasting and prayer may be necessary and useful in helping us gain victory over our own stubborn flesh and cast out the spirit of unbelief that blocks God's power from flowing through us. It is this kind of unbelief that goes out only "by prayer and fasting." It is also worth mentioning that some manuscripts do not contain the statement about prayer and fasting at all, which is why many Bible translations have left it out completely. Any way you look at it, faith is the key to powerful prayer. This is the point Jesus made in this story.

In Matthew 9:25, when Jairus's daughter died, Jesus had to send everyone out of the room before He could raise her from the dead. Why didn't He allow all those scornful skeptics to see the miracle with their own eyes? Because He had to cast the unbelief out. Peter did the same thing in Acts 9:40: *"But Peter sent them all out and knelt down and prayed, and turning to the body, he said, 'Tabitha, arise.' And she opened her eyes, and when she saw Peter, she sat up"*. Jesus taught His disciples an important lesson:

Cast the spirit of unbelief out, and nothing will be able to stand against you. Demons, death, and even the most formidable mountains will obey your command!

GOD'S BASKET

Investors often "diversify" their investments because if one venture doesn't work out, they want to have something else to fall back on. So, a common idiom in the business world is, "Don't put all your eggs in one basket." That means, don't put all your resources into one investment, because if one of your "baskets" breaks and all your "eggs" are in it, you will lose everything. You see, if you are holding back some of your "eggs," it means you are not 100 percent confident that a particular basket will hold. You may be 50 percent confident or even 99 percent confident, but that small percentage of apprehension is what I am calling "unbelief." So how do you know when you've gotten rid of all the unbelief? When you've put all of your eggs into God's basket.

Early in ministry I came to a crossroads where I had to decide to go in one direction or another. I essentially had to choose between a situation that offered security, financially and otherwise, and following the call of God with all its risks and unknowns. I had an inward conviction that I had to give myself fully to one or the other, but I didn't want to let go of either option. In prayer I said, "Lord, I don't want to be foolish and put all of my eggs in one basket." Then I heard the Lord speak. He said, "You can trust my basket." I have seen this to be true.

God's basket is the best one; it is fully reliable and never breaks.

When Hernando Cortez, the famous Spanish explorer, arrived in Mexico's Harbor of Vera Cruz in 1519, he faced overwhelming odds. Before him lay the mighty Aztec empire with its vast armies. But Cortez had only about 600 men with him. They were far from home in a strange land; all the odds were stacked hopelessly against them. Cortez knew his men would always have one eye on the ships, longing for home. He knew that in the back of their minds they would always be considering the highly attractive alternative of retreat. He knew that if these men were divided in heart or mind the mission would surely fail.

So, Cortez did something unthinkable. He ordered all eleven ships in their fleet to be burned. When the men stood on the shore and watched their only escape route going up in flames, it was a defining moment. There was no longer any possibility of turning back. They would either conquer or die. This consummate and unmitigated commitment unlocked unbelievable potential that gave them the power to succeed where all those before them had failed.

James 1:8 says, *"A double minded man is unstable in all his ways."* You will never really succeed at anything if you are halfway in and halfway out. If God has called you, it is not necessary to have a "backup plan." You don't need to hedge your bets. You don't need to hold some of your eggs back "just in case." Cast out the unbelief, put all of your eggs in God's basket, burn your ships, and give yourself to Him and His plan, body, soul and spirit.

When you are 100 percent committed and there is no turning back, you will break into a level of effectiveness and power that you've never experienced before.

You will succeed where others have failed. You will overcome in the face of overwhelming odds. Mountains will move for you, and nothing will be impossible for you.

NO FEAR OF THE FUTURE

One of the areas of greatest difficulty for so many of God's people is simple obedience. We are often like sheep – prone to wander and amazingly stupid. We are often like donkeys – stubborn and willful. We are often like peacocks – proud and vain. We are quick to analyze and rationalize but slow to obey. We are masters of procrastination and experts at justification. Making excuses comes naturally to us, but simple obedience seems so difficult.

"And now, Israel, what does the LORD your God require of you, but to fear the LORD your God, to walk in all His ways and to love Him, to serve the LORD your God with all your heart and with all your soul, and to keep the commandments of the LORD and His statutes which I command you today for your good?" (Deuteronomy 10:12-13)

Notice that God's commands are not given to make us miserable; they are for our own good! This might sound like a cliché, but please do not dismiss it and simply go on to the next paragraph. Stop to consider this thought for a moment. God is all knowing and all wise. He knows the future. He knows the past. He can see what is ahead in your life and in the lives of everyone around you. He knows what is going to happen in the economy, in politics, and on the world stage. When He speaks, He is giving you insider information for your advantage, and your obedience is the most profitable thing you could do for yourself and your family.

Those who are obedient to the Lord have no need to fear the future.

I could point to many examples in my own life of times when God spoke to me about something, but because obeying required some level of personal sacrifice, I struggled and wrestled in my own heart and mind, sometimes for far too long. In the end I discovered that His instructions were meant to save me mountains of heartache, pain, and expense.

If we could only learn to obey, we would be fulfilled, happy, and blessed in every way.

John H. Sammis's famous hymn says it well: Trust and obey, for there's no other way to be happy in Jesus, but to trust and obey. 1 Samuel 15:22 says, *"Has the Lord as much delight in burnt offerings and sacrifices as in obeying the voice of the Lord? Behold, to obey is better than sacrifice, and to heed than the fat of rams."* There is no alternative to obedience – not even sacrifices, invocations, or tears. When God speaks, there is only one appropriate response – immediate, unquestioning obedience.

WHAT IS IN YOUR HAND?

When God called Moses to deliver the children of Israel out of Egypt, Moses was thoroughly overwhelmed. His mind was filled with questions, and he could not even imagine how he would begin to accomplish such a feat. He began to bombard God with questions, concerns, and objections, but God did not say, "Don't worry, Moses. This is what I'm going to do. First, I'm going to turn the waters of the Nile into blood. Then I'll send a plague of frogs, followed by a plague of lice, followed by a plague of flies. Then I'll kill the livestock, send boils, hail and locusts, then follow that up with darkness and death of the firstborn. Once you're out of Egypt, I'll part the Red Sea and lead you through the wilderness with a pillar of cloud by day and a pillar of fire by night." I'm sure such a detailed revelation of God's plan would have been a great comfort to Moses. Instead when Moses asked all his frantic questions about how

God would deliver His people, God responded with a question of His own. "Moses, what is in your hand?" And Moses replied, "A rod."

Think for a minute about the absurdity of what God was asking Moses to do. He was sending this fugitive vagabond into the most powerful empire in the world to deliver His people. And all Moses had as ammunition was a stick! Through the whole Exodus saga – all the miracles, wonders, and epic, world-changing exploits – Moses had nothing more in his hand than a stick! But when Moses did what he knew to do, when he used what was in his hand, the rest of the story began to unfold, each event triggering the next like a succession of dominoes leading all the way to the Promised Land.

Right now, people all over the world are worried because of one crisis or another. Many of them have lost jobs, financial resources and security. People have lots of questions and concerns about the future. If you are feeling uncertain, maybe this is a word from the Lord for you.

Take an inventory of your life today to see what is in your hand right now. It may be people, relationships, interests, opportunities, thoughts, or dreams. Chances are that the seeds of your future have already been sown into the soil of your life. Ask God to give you the wisdom to discern them; then have the diligence to water them and the patience to wait for the harvest.

And don't worry, if God can make a way for an entire nation using only a stick, He can surely make a way for you!

WALK IN GOD'S POWER

You may have heard that a virus can't live in certain physical conditions such as soap and water, alcohol-based sanitizers, and high temperatures. The shell of the virus disintegrates in those conditions, making it impossible for it to enter into, human cells.

Just as a virus has no chance of survival in soapy water, sickness has no chance of survival in the glory of God. In Acts 5:14-16, we read that the measure of God's manifest glory was resting upon Peter in a great way: *"And believers were increasingly added to the Lord, multitudes of both men and women, so that they brought the sick out into the streets and laid them on beds and couches, that at least the shadow of Peter passing by might fall on some of them. Also a multitude gathered from the surrounding cities to Jerusalem, bringing sick people and those who were tormented by unclean spirits, and they were all healed."*

It is incredible to think we can walk in such a measure of the manifest glory of God that no sickness or demonic power would be able to stand in our presence! God in His splendor can and does move into the natural realm of human existence where He can be experienced by people.

A lost and dying world longs to see the Gospel, experience the Gospel, and be touched and healed by the power of the Gospel. They want to do more than to just hear the Gospel with their ears. A person who hears the Gospel should have an experience that needs an explanation, not just an explanation of something in need of an experience! The Gospel must be a life-altering encounter. The manifestation of God's glory is not just something that happened in biblical times. Right now, because of the prayers of God's people, faith in His Word, and the declaration of the Gospel, we are seeing God's glory manifested all over the world every day.

People are healed every day! With God, the supernatural is natural and the impossible is possible! Christianity should be a supernatural existence from beginning to end, and the demonstration of God's power should be the norm. Be a light in the darkness. Do not cower in fear like those in the world whose only hope is in science, medicine, politics and economics. You are a child of God. All the resources of heaven are at your disposal. The power at work in you is the same power God exerted when He raised Christ from the dead (Ephesians 1:20). Rise up and walk in that power in Jesus' name!

FAITH FRIGHTENS SATAN

I had an experience during one of our gospel campaigns in Africa that gave me a revelation. We were to use our big tent in Green Valley, South Africa. The team was ready to pitch the canvas tabernacle, which, at that time, held ten thousand people, African style. With great anticipation, I was counting the hours to the first meeting. Then the tent manager phoned. "The ground is too soft," he said. "If there is any wind or rain the anchors and masts will lose their grip, and the tent could collapse. Wet soil will not support it." His question then was should he go ahead and pitch the tent. My mind was working fast on this question. It would be a terrible thing if it all went wrong. I prayed to the Lord in my heart while I thought. Then wonderful, divine assurance flooded my mind. "Go ahead," I replied. "In the name of Jesus, it is not going to rain or storm." On that instruction, the tent went up.

We had a wonderful start. Night after night, the tent was packed with people hungry for God. Then one afternoon, while I was kneeling in prayer in my caravan parked near the tent, I looked up and saw a mighty thunderstorm filling the western sky and heading in our direction. Have you ever seen an African storm, which fills the air with water? The clouds, like masses of pitch-black curly hair, were being tossed by the storm within them. "Here comes your catastrophe," something inside me said. Then I heard the voice of the Holy Spirit answering that fear, telling me what to do: "Go and rebuke the devil!" I went out and walked aggressively in the direction of the imminent storm. Lifting my finger and pointing, I said, "Devil, I want to talk to you in the name of Jesus. If you destroy this tent of mine, I am going to trust God for a tent three times this size!" I looked, and at that moment, something incredible happened – the clouds parted. They began to make a detour away from and around the tent. The menace was over!

The clouds and rain never reached us, and the tent stood firm for the rest of the gospel campaign. How great our God is! Then this wonderful truth hit me harder than any thunderbolt that the storm could have hurled at us: Faith frightens Satan! My faith had scared off the devil. He probably had enough to worry about already, with this tent of ours, and faith for a bigger one shook him.

"Demons tremble," the Bible declares in James 2:19. When we arise with living faith and tackle the opposition in God's strength, our faith terrorizes the arch-terrorist, Satan.

"Submit to God. Resist the devil and he will flee from you," the Bible declares (James 4:7).

The Bible also instructs us to resist our adversary, the devil: *"Resist him, firm in your faith"* (1 Peter 5:9). This is fact. John testified, *"I write to you, young men, because you have overcome the wicked one"* (1 John 2:13). With faith in God, even *"the lame take the prey"* (Isaiah 33:23).

My tent episode was not quite over, for something unsettling nagged at my heart. "What if the devil misunderstood my words?" I wondered. The thought kept coming back to me. Therefore, I decided to make the issue clear. I spoke to the devil in the name of Jesus once more, telling him, "I make no bargains with you. Just because you withdrew the wind and the rain does not mean that I made an agreement with you about not having a bigger tent. The bigger tent comes anyway." We are not to negotiate with the devil – we are to cast him out. That is all that the Bible tells us to do. Keep repeating to yourself – faith frightens Satan, faith frightens Satan, faith frightens Satan! This truth will change you from negative to positive.

In Jesus, you are the victor, not the victim.

Satan is the victim, because Jesus crushed the serpent's head.

GET HEAVEN'S PERSPECTIVE

Isaiah, chapter 6:1-3, gives us a perspective from the throne room of the Lord. *"In the year that King Uzziah died I saw the Lord sitting upon a throne, high and lifted up; and the train of his robe filled the temple. Above him stood the seraphim. Each had six wings: with two he covered his face, and with two he covered his feet, and with two he flew. And one called to another and said, "Holy, holy, holy is the Lord of hosts; the whole earth is full of his glory!" The seraphim used their third pair of wings to fly. As they flew, they cried out, saying, "Holy, holy, holy is the LORD of Hosts; the whole earth is full of His glory."* They flew and sang. It was worship on the very highest scale! The beat of their wings was music. The amazing thing about these heavenly beings is that they did not cry, "Love, love, love," or "Peace, peace, peace," but a triune "Holy, holy, holy is the LORD of hosts."

The zenith of praise and the highest form of worship are always connected with the holiness and glory of God.

How could these angels say that the whole earth is full of God's glory? Had they never heard of the heathen and atheistic empires, of war, hatred, greed, and suffering? Had they never heard of sickness and disease? Yes, of course they had, but they saw them from a higher viewpoint as they flew before the throne. They had God's perspective, not the human view. Soaring above the earthly scene, with the total situation revealed, they burst into rapturous exclamation. Scanning horizons beyond the sight of earth dwellers, the skies of all tomorrows, they sang, "The whole earth is full of His glory."

If you're feeling overwhelmed by what is going on in the world today; if you're feeling dwarfed by the mountain of circumstances you find yourself in, you need to go up and get the throne perspective!

Get the throne perspective of the world – get the throne perspective of your life!

The Bible says Believers are seated in heavenly places in Christ Jesus (Ephesians 2:6). What is your angle? Do you have a molehill aspect or an Everest view? You ascend to God's throne and thus His perspective when you praise and worship.

You see, praise lifts you! Doubt, fear, and murmuring only serve as weights on your back and boots of lead on your feet, but in worship, we contemplate the throne, the power of the Lord, and His holiness! There we rest under His protection.

In the throne room, Isaiah was equipped, sent, and cleansed with the altar fire in order to be God's servant with perfect integrity. Oh, glory to God! When we serve the Lord with purity of motive, rejoicing in His presence before His throne, we are invincible, immune, impregnable! Trouble starts when get caught up in the cares of this world. When we allow fear to overwhelm us, we lose the throne perspective. However, elevated by worship to the third dimension, our character will be armor-plated; our fears will subside, and our faith will be strengthened, in the presence of the Lord of Hosts!

DUNAMIS POWER

Reinhard Bonnke once said, "Man needs God but God needs man. When the two come together for God's purposes, anything becomes possible." The supernatural agreement through faith between Almighty God and a man or a woman who knows how to pray is more powerful than a thermonuclear bomb! It is a partnership between heaven and earth that is exercised when God's people agree with the purposes of God and pray those purposes into being in the earthly realm. This largely unrecognized truth from God's Word is what James 5:16 was referring to when it says, *"The effectual fervent prayer of a righteous man* [or woman] *availeth much."* The Amplified Bible translates this same Scripture, *"The earnest* [heartfelt, continued] *prayer of a righteous man makes tremendous power available* [dynamic in its working]."

The word "power" in this scripture comes from the Greek word dunamis which properly translated means power, inherent ability, capability, ability to perform anything. 2 Timothy 1:7 says, *"For God has not given us a spirit of fear, but of power and of love and of a sound mind."* We've been given a spirit of dunamis power!

The Bible teaches us that when we pray, we have the ability to engage the power of heaven in our circumstances and in the events of the earth. Prayer prayed in faith has the power to destroy the devil's schemes and make the way for every barrier to be shattered, every gate to be blown open, and for God's blessings to flow without interruption. That's power!

As long as the enemy can keep the people of God afraid and convinced that they are powerless against the circumstances that they face, their impact in the earth will be anemic and of little influence. When the people of God begin to pray with the realization of the power they've been given, Satan will tuck tail and run!

PARTNERING WITH GOD IN PRAYER

God wants to answer our prayers of intercession more than we want Him to answer them. Intercession is not a human invention – it is God's idea! He has called us to partner with Him in prayer. God longs to reveal His great power in cities, regions, and nations in order that multitudes of people may be saved. He wants to reveal Himself to those who walk in darkness that they may behold the glorious light of the Gospel and come to Him. He longs to see people set free, healed, and restored! He longs to see hell plundered and heaven populated! He has given His people (the Church) all the tools we need through prayer and faith in the mighty name of Jesus to see that happen, if we will only use them as He has intended. He has put into our hands the keys of the kingdom that are capable of unlocking the treasure houses of heaven, shattering the chains off of nations, destroying yokes, and breaking curses.

In our mass Gospel Campaigns where hundreds of thousands attend each meeting, multitudes of sick and needy people gather for prayer. It is physically impossible to lay hands on each person., but we have made an incredible discovery.

There are no limitations with God!

When we pray over the gigantic crowd, miracles and healings begin to pop up like popcorn, and from the front to the back the power of God flows equally to all. We have seen people get healed, delivered, and baptized in the fire of the Holy Ghost! All of this happens through the simple power of faith and prayer. You must understand, you have this same secret weapon!

JESUS, YOUR HEALER

Jesus healed multitudes – that was His mission. He came to heal as well as to save. He did not come from glory to earth only for those people who happened to be alive during that period in history. He did not come to bring relief merely to a few thousand people. That was only the beginning! *"Then he healed many who were sick with various diseases, and cast out many demons; and he did not allow the demons to speak, because they knew him... And again He began to teach by the sea. And a great multitude was gathered to him, so that he got into a boat and sat in it on the sea; and the whole multitude was on the land facing the sea. Then he taught them many things by parables."* (Mark 1:34; 4:1-9)

The Bible says that it was what "Jesus began to do." By his deeds, he showed us what he wanted to do, so that we can see what he was – and still is – like. He came to heal them so that he could heal you! People living in the days of Jesus' earthly ministry possibly thought of Jesus more as a healer than anything else. He set out to heal. That was Jesus. He did not wait for the sick to come to him – he often went to them. The apostle Peter actually said that Jesus went around for that very purpose. Healing was a major part of his mission, and Jesus said God sent him to do those very works.

If a man spends eight years or more studying to become a doctor, when he has finished his studies, he will open a surgery to treat sick people. It would be ridiculous for a doctor not to practice after all his efforts to qualify. We read in Matthew: "He himself took our infirmities and bore our sicknesses." That is a quotation from the prophet Isaiah about the crucifixion. Christ bore your pains and your sins in his own body on the cross.

If Jesus died for you, it is not too much to expect him to heal you!

"Jesus went about all Galilee, teaching in their synagogues, preaching the gospel of the kingdom, and healing all kinds of sickness and all kinds of disease among the people."
(Matthew 4:23)

Know that Jesus included your healing in His purpose on Earth and accept His gift with thanksgiving!

APPLY THE BLOOD!

When Jesus walked on earth, and delivered people from the oppression of Satan, that old deceiver watched him. The blind saw, and cripples walked. Christ was destroying the works of the devil systematically. Satan ground his teeth with rage, and plotted to destroy the Lord Jesus Christ. He inspired evil men to crucify Christ. He gloated as they nailed down those wonderful hands of mercy. "Those hands will give me no more trouble," he thought. "It is all over!" What a mistake Satan made. The very blood he caused to be spilled now breaks the stranglehold of Satan upon men and women everywhere, especially for you and me!

In the first chapter of Revelation it says, *"In the midst of the seven lampstands one like the Son of Man, clothed with a garment down to the feet and girded about the chest with a golden band... He laid his right hand on me, saying to me, 'Do not be afraid; I am the First and the Last. I am he who lives, and was dead, and behold I am alive forevermore. Amen. And I have the keys of Hades and of death.'"* (Revelation 1:13-18)

An atheist once challenged me on a television program; "I do not believe that there is any power in the blood of Jesus. The blood of Jesus has been around for 2,000 years, and if there was any power in it – as you claim – the world would not be in such a sorry state." I replied, "Sir, there is also plenty of soap around, and yet many people are still dirty. Soap does not make a person clean by just being around, not even if he works in a soap factory. If you want to know what soap can do – you have to take it, and apply it personally. Then you will see! That is how it is with the blood of Jesus. It is not enough to know about the blood, sing about it, or preach about it. I now challenge you, sir," I said, "apply the blood of Jesus to your sinful life, and you will join hundreds of millions of people all over the world who sing and say: 'There is power, power, wonder-working power, in the precious blood of the Lamb.'"

JESUS IS REAL!

If we know Jesus is real, why do we live as if He did not exist? If there is a Father in heaven, why do we behave as if we were orphans? If there is a Savior, why do we cringe in fear and misery? If there is a Healer, why do we not ask Him for healing?

Jesus says,

"Do not be afraid; only believe." (Mark 5:36)

If things go wrong, they can also go right! If the devil can be effective, how much more so can God! Faith is supposed to prove its worth in times of great need. For so many believers, that is precisely when it grinds to a screeching halt. For them, faith only works in blessed Christian meetings; or when everything is going right. To put it figuratively, they wear their life preservers only so long as they are on the ship, and toss them off as soon as they fall into the sea! How ridiculous can you get? Let's toss off fear, not our faith! Let's embrace the living reality of Jesus Christ in our life today!

Faith may follow a process like this:

1. **BELIEVING SOMETHING IS TRUE.**
   Believing that there is a God is not enough.
   The devil believes the same thing – but it's a start.

2. **BELIEVING A PERSON IS GENUINE.**
   Many believe that Jesus was a good man.
   ut He claimed to be much more – the Savior of the world!

3. **BELIEVING IN GOD'S POWER.**
   Many believed in Christ's healing power.
   But they did not all make him their Lord and Savior

4. **BELIEVING AS TRUST.**
   Trust makes things personal. We trust people we feel will not fail us.

5. **BELIEVING IN CHRIST.**
   This is real faith. It is complete surrender to Jesus!

Allow Jesus to take over every area of your life! Completely surrender to Him today. Romans 8:2 says, *"For the law of the Spirit of life in Christ Jesus has made me free from the law of sin and death."*

Live your life in the fullness of Christ Jesus, and you will be an overcomer through Him!

SEEK AND YOU WILL FIND

We will only find God if we truly want him. As He says in the Bible: *"I love those who love me, and those who seek me diligently will find me... Surely you shall call a nation you do not know, and nations who do not know you shall run to you, because of the LORD your God, and the Holy One of Israel; for he has glorified you. Seek the LORD while he may be found, call upon him while he is near."* (Proverbs 8:17; Isaiah 55:5-6)

And He makes this cast-iron promise: *"For I know the thoughts that I think toward you, says the LORD, thoughts of peace and not of evil, to give you a future and a hope. Then you will call upon me and go and pray to me, and I will listen to you. And you will seek me and find me, when you search for me with all your heart."* (Jeremiah 29:11-13)

At the point of our deepest need, the Good News of Jesus Christ cuts in! Jesus saw his life as a rescue mission. He said that he had come *"to seek and to save that which was lost."* He also said that his death was no accident – because he had come to die, *"For the Son of Man did not come to be served, but to serve, and to give his life a ransom for many."* (Mark 10:45)

Is peace our deepest need? No, although Christ has provided that also. *"Peace I leave with you, my peace I give to you; not as the world gives do I give to you. Let not your heart be troubled, neither let it be afraid."* (John 14:27)

The Good News of Jesus Christ is our deepest need. All the unrest, all the heartache and loneliness, all the pain and despair, all the sin and corruption, is replaced by the Gospel. This is the plan that God had in mind for us all along – a rightful relationship with him, in which all of our needs are satisfied. Meaning Jesus is all we really need! Make that your strongest desire today – that you are always in right relationship with Christ, because then you can change the world!

THE FAITH FUSE

Faith has neither bulk nor weight, for it is something that you do. Jesus spoke of "faith as a mustard seed," referring to something tiny, but with huge potential. Perhaps today, he might speak of faith as a fuse. Tiny as it is, it transmits the awesome power generated in power stations to our homes. Without it, every appliance is useless, unable to draw from that power.

Our faith – however small we think it may be – can accomplish great things.

"Another parable he put forth to them, saying: 'The kingdom of heaven is like a mustard seed, which a man took and sowed in his field, which indeed is the least of all the seeds; but when

it is grown it is greater than the herbs and becomes a tree, so that the birds of the air come and nest in its branches.'" (Matthew 13:31-32)

As believers, we know what we believe, and in whom we believe. Believing tests us.

Taking God's Word at face value, accepting its divine authority, we plug into the very Source!

Faith is the vital link. By it, the energies of heaven flow into the world... and into your life. *"Believe on the Lord Jesus Christ, and you will be saved, you and your household."* (Acts 16:31)

The greatness of God, the work of Christ, or the Word of God, without faith as small as a fuse wire, is unavailable. The circuit is broken. Once connected, the fuse itself cannot help, but shows the effects of the power surging through it. It warms up! Faith makes us dynamic, exuberant, excited! Allow the fuse of faith to activate your life today. *"What does it profit, my brethren, if someone says he has faith but does not have works? Can faith save him?... Thus also faith by itself, if it does not have works, is dead. But someone will say, 'You have faith, and I have works.' Show me your faith without your works, and I will show you my faith by my works."* (James 2:14-19)

Take God's word at face value!
Accepting its divine authority is connecting to the very source of life!

FREE FROM FEAR

"Whenever I am afraid, I will trust in You"
(Psalms 56:3).

This is the time to trust in the Lord. In fact, it is always time to trust in Him. Unfortunately, some are by nature nervous and prone to fear, depression, and even panic. The writer of Psalm 42 seems to have been temperamentally afflicted as well, but faith came to his aid. He said, *"My tears have been my food day and night... why are you cast down, O my soul? And why are you disquieted within me?"* He seems to have no rational explanation for his depression. However, he knew where to get strength. He spoke to himself,

"Hope in God, for I shall yet praise Him"
(Psalms 42:5).

This illustrates a major lesson – faith is not a feeling. When danger comes, fear is inevitable. Fear is a feeling. When our bodily chemistry sets up a sense of impending disaster or we suffer heavy blows and our circumstances are oppressive and dark or when pain and illness sit with us at the fireside – fear and alarm come as a natural cause and effect. That's when we have a choice. We choose to address the fear with our faith in Jesus! The moment we make that choice, faith takes over and releases us from the hook of fear. With God, fear will not stop us. We overcome. If we are believers, nothing can alter it, no matter what hammers and bruises us.

Jesus said His followers were to give their lives for Him, but *"not a hair of your head shall be lost"* (Luke 21:18). You – the real you – believes God. The sea's surface is ruffled, but the depths are still. Faith operates without emotional reactions. It secretly imparts strength of mind and peace of spirit, so you do not go under but over. Faith gets us off the hook of fear! Faith is not just for Sunday and good times, but for life – and whatever perils may come with it. Faith is not just for transplanting mountains (see Matthew 21:21) but for living! God gives us grace to live a life of faith! And we choose to believe, because the just will live by faith!

"IT IS I;
DO NOT BE AFRAID"

Let's examine a passage in John chapter 6: *"Now when evening came, His disciples went down to the sea, got into the boat, and went over the sea toward Capernaum. And it was already dark, and Jesus had not come to them. Then the sea arose because a great wind was blowing. So when they had rowed about three or four miles, they saw Jesus walking on the sea and drawing near the boat; and they were afraid. But He said to them, "It is I; do not be afraid." Then they willingly received Him into the boat, and immediately the boat was at the land where they were going."* (John 6:16-20)

The disciples were rowing hard against wind and current in the darkness, when suddenly they saw a phantom figure gliding across the churning surface of the lake. Their fears doubled. Hardy men as they were, they shouted with terror. Then, above the howl of the winds, cutting across the spume came Christ's voice, *"It is I; do not be afraid."* (John 6:20)

Jesus was a carpenter or builder, not a seaman, but they knew that *"with Christ in the vessel they can smile at the storm."* He was and is the conqueror of devils and darkness. Until then, they were alone. (See John 6:22) That is what the multitude noticed. Jesus had such tremendous stature in their eyes that when the disciples went without Him, they were alone. They were a dozen weather-hardened fishermen together, boatmen, experts on familiar waters, but because Jesus was not with them, they were alone! They were worse than alone. They were lonely and in the dark.

If all of the nearly eight billion people on this planet had no Jesus, we would all be alone together, in the dark. This world would be as dreadful and lonely as winter in the ice-clad Antarctic. But He is there! Or rather – here! We are not alone in an unfriendly universe. We have a Friend. *"I go to prepare a place for you... I will come again... that where I am, there you may be also."* (John 14:3) Meanwhile? *"Lo, I am with you always, even to the end of the age."* (Matthew 28:20)

He is here! He is with us!
Jesus relieves the anxiety of us all.

Even in a waterlogged old boat, clutched by hissing waves, the disciples were immediately relieved when Jesus said, *"It is I, be not afraid."* The words recorded in the Greek (ego eimi) are literally "I am." Because He is, we can feel safe!

"Yea, though I walk through the valley of the shadow of death, I will fear no evil; for You are with me." (Psalms 23:4) That is all we need to know.

Then John adds that final touch: *"Then they willingly received Him into the boat, and immediately the boat was at the land where they were going."* (John 6:21) No doubt they were more than willing to take Him into the boat, but Mark 6:48 says He *"would have passed them by."* In other words, it was up to them. If they were willing, He would be with them. That is always the way of Jesus. He waits for our invitation.

Give the Lord an invitation into
your situation.
He's the light in the darkness.
He's the answer to every problem and
He can calm any storm.
With Him, we have nothing to fear.

References

Day 1: Slaying Dragons
Day 2: Slaying Dragons
Day 3: Faith: The link with God's Power
Day 4: God's Promises for Hope and Healing. Faith: The Link with God's Power
Day 5: Taking Action
Day 6: Faith: The Link with God's Power
Day 7: Faith: The Link with God's Power
Day 8: Evangelism by Fire
Day 9: Evangelism by Fire
Day 10: Evangelism by Fire
Day 11: Evangelism by Fire
Day 12: Evangelism by Fire
Day 13: Slaying Dragons
Day 14: Faith: The Link with God's Power
Day 15: God's Promises for Healing & Hope
Day 16: Faith: The Link with God's Power
Day 17: Evangelism by Fire
Day 18: Slaying Dragons
Day 19: Evangelism by Fire
Day 20: Evangelism by Fire
Day 21: Faith: The Link with God's Power
Day 22: Faith: The Link with God's Power
Day 23: Faith: The Link with God's Power
Day 24: God's Promises for Healing & Hope
Day 25: Evangelism by Fire
Day 26: God's Promises for Healing and Hope
Day 27: Evangelism by Fire
Day 28: Surviving Your Wilderness
Day 29: Surviving Your Wilderness
Day 30: Surviving Your Wilderness
Day 31: Unlocking the Miraculous
Day 32: Live Before You Die
Day 33: Unlocking the Miraculous
Day 34: Surviving Your Wilderness
Day 35: Live Before You Die
Day 36: Unlocking the Miraculous
Day 37: Surviving Your Wilderness
Day 38: Taking Action
Day 39: Faith: The Link with God's Power
Day 40: Taking Action
Day 41: Surviving Your Wilderness
Day 42: Live Before You Die
Day 43: Live Before You Die

Day 44: Live Before You Die

Day 45: Live Before You Die

Day 46: Live Before You Die

Day 47: Live Before You Die

Day 48: Live Before You Die

Day 49: Unlocking the Miraculous Through Faith and Prayer

Day 50: Evangelism by Fire

Day 51: Evangelism by Fire

Day 52: Unlocking the Miraculous

Day 53: Unlocking the Miraculous

Day 54: Daily Fire Devotional

Day 55: Daily Fire Devotional

Day 56: Daily Fire Devotional

Day 57: Daily Fire Devotional

Day 58: Daily Fire Devotional

Day 59: Faith: The Link with God's Power

Day 60: Faith: The Link with God's Power

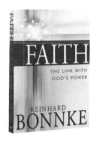

SLAYING DRAGONS

The supernatural realm is very real, and it directly impacts our day-to-day lives. Often spiritual battles lie behind our everyday struggles. Though the spiritual world is invisible, we are not unaware of the enemy's schemes.

With doctrinally sound, practical teaching, Slaying Dragons shows how the demonic realm fits into orthodox thoughts on salvation, redemption, and kingdom life. Daniel Kolenda demystifies spiritual warfare to shine light on what the enemy is doing in readers' lives and what they can do to slay every dragon they encounter. It also contains real-world examples of encounters with spiritual darkness, demonstrating examples of how *"the light shines in the darkness, and the darkness has not overcome it"* (John 1:5, NIV).

Slaying Dragons will show readers what the enemy is trying to accomplish and how they can slay every dragon they encounter—in their lives and in the world.

Faith: The link with God's Power

Some believe that simply having faith is an entitlement to blessing and prosperity. Others believe that faith in oneself is all that is needed in life. Still others contend that faith is a cosmic force that breeds superhuman, super-spiritual, invincible people.

In this book, Reinhard Bonnke reveals the truth about faith towards God, drawing from his many years of personal study and experience.

SURVIVING YOUR WILDERNESS

The wilderness is an untamed place, a most difficult season for the human soul. But it can become the source of the greatest spiritual reward. As we have seen in the history of Israel, as well as the life of Jesus Christ, God establishes His greatest works in the wilderness.

In God's wisdom, life comes out of death, glory out of suffering, streams out of the desert. All of this happens so that God alone may be glorified for His marvelous handiwork in the lives of those who dare to be fashioned in barren places.

UNLOCKING THE MIRACULOUS

Unlocking the Miraculous contains power-filled chapters such as Prayer that Opens Doors, Praying Under an Open Heaven and Prayer that Releases the Miraculous and much more. It is studded with spiritual truths and the insights of a man who knows that there are no limits to what God can do if we, his children, come before him in prayer. For the author, the only thing worse than prayer-less-ness is prayer without expectation. Intercession is not a human invention; it is God's idea. He has called us to partner with him in prayer, believing in faith. This book is for those who desire to enter into this divine partnership and join the prayer revolution.

LIVE BEFORE YOU DIE

God has a plan for everyone. Do you know yours?

Before you were even born, He had a dream for your life. But sometimes it is hard to know what that dream is, or how to fulfil it.

Daniel Kolenda helps you answer the universal question: Where do I belong? Drawing from Scripture and his own experiences, he gives practical advice to help you tune into God's call, revealing:

- Seven secrets to discovering God's will
- How to start moving in the right direction
- What to do when God says wait
- How to stay in the will of God

Whether your journey takes you to the mission field or medical school, whether you become a construction worker, stay-at-home mom, businessman, teacher, chef, or pastor – discovering God's will for your life is not a matter of determining what you want but what God wants. It is a spiritual quest of the utmost significance.

DAILY FIRE DEVOTIONAL
(MARK MY WORD)

Features a brief, daily motivational message; a Scripture verse for the day; related Bible passages; a "Daily Fire" encouragement to carry you through the day; and a verse plan to help you read through the entire Bible in one year. It is a collection of dynamic devotionals from the powerful writings of Evangelist Reinhard Bonnke. With its simple, convenient, easy-to-read format, you can take this book anywhere and plunge in at any point. Read specific indexed selections focused on a particular topic or read it chronologically as your personal daily Bible reading program. Much more than a daily devotional, this book will give you a passion for lost souls and motivate you to be a soul winner.

MORE PRODUCTS AND ORDER
shop.cfan.uk

Scan the QR code

Stay in touch with us!

We as the CfaN team truly value our mission partners, friends and supporters.

We look forward to hearing from you if you have a question, a prayer request, or a testimony to share, or if you need encouragement.

Scan the QR code

CfaN
**CHRIST
FOR ALL NATIONS**

Highway House,
250 Coombs Road,
Halesowen, West Midlands
B62 8AA, UK

Tel. +44 (121) 602 2000

info@cfan.org.uk
cfan.org.uk
danielkolenda.com

 cfanuk
evangelistdanielkolenda

 cfanuk
evangelistkolenda

 cfanuk
danielkolenda

Scan the QR code

Mailings

We will gladly send you physical
mailings with regular reports of
our African events, encouraging
Bible studies, prayer initiatives
for you to join, new and
interesting products, and the
latest news about CfaN.

Newsletter

Our online newsletter always
keeps you up-to-date. Of
particular interest is our "CfaN
Top News" directly from our
Gospel Campaigns in Africa with
relevant reports, pictures, video
clips and healing testimonies.
Don't miss out! Just enter your
e-mail address on the website.